D0172090

THE SOUL OF A HERO

THE
SOUL
OF A
HERO

BECOMING THE MAN OF STRENGTH AND
PURPOSE YOU WERE CREATED TO BE

STEPHEN ARTERBURN
& DAVID STOOP

WITH B. A. JOHNSON

TYNDALE
MOMENTUM®

The Tyndale nonfiction imprint

Visit Tyndale online at tyndale.com.

Visit Tyndale Momentum online at tyndalemomentum.com.

TYNDALE, Tyndale's quill logo, *Tyndale Momentum*, and the Tyndale Momentum logo are registered trademarks of Tyndale House Ministries. Tyndale Momentum is the nonfiction imprint of Tyndale House Publishers, Carol Stream, Illinois.

The Soul of a Hero: Becoming the Man of Strength and Purpose You Were Created to Be

Designed by Mark Anthony Lane II

Authors are represented by the literary agency of WordServe Literary Group, www.wordserveliterary.com.

The stories in this book are true, but in some cases we have changed the names and identifying details of the people involved to protect their privacy.

For information about special discounts for bulk purchases, please contact Tyndale House Publishers at csresponse@tyndale.com, or call 1-855-277-9400.

ISBN 978-1-4964-1371-0

Printed in the United States of America

27 26 25 24 23 22 21
7   6   5   4   3   2   1

Contents

Heroes at Heart

After a combined seventy years of helping men overcome everything from feeling aimless and without purpose to private addictions and a myriad of complex male issues, we have come to believe that a high percentage of guys are lost, off track, and disconnected from their true calling: *to be a hero.*

Be honest now: Does the word *hero* resonate with you, or does it miss the mark, leaving you feeling cold and disconnected?

Maybe you're thinking, *What's heroic about my life?*

Well, here are four things you need to know:

1. God created every man to have a heroic heart, soul, and mind. It's part of the image of God in us.
2. There's a heroic path and purpose for *every* man, regardless of temperament, personality, or calling.
3. You have an enemy who will do everything he can to undermine your heroic journey.

4. If you're willing to fight (which is part of the heroic journey), you can uncover your heroic heart and pursue your heroic purpose.

So, who is this heroic man you're designed to be? We'll answer that question more fully over the next seven chapters, but here's a working definition to get you started:

A *hero* is a man who knows his place in God's eyes.

A *hero* is a man who knows his purpose on earth.

A *hero* is a man who enjoys healthy relationships.

A *hero* is a man who lives with a sense of meaning.

A *hero* is a man who lives with a spirit of adventure.

In other words, a hero is a man who is spiritually secure, strongly connected, and certain of his purpose. In the Bible, we see that heroism is built on strong character, courageous action, unselfishness, and faithfulness, even in the worst of circumstances.

Seriously, what guy wouldn't want to live that way?

As we go along, we'll take a deeper look at what it means to be a hero, and we'll explore how the hero within us evolves as we journey from boyhood to manhood.

In the meantime, let's approach it from a different angle.

If you're at all like us, you're able to grasp deeper meanings more quickly and easily through stories you can relate to. So let's begin with three stories that illustrate the soul of a hero.

Eli began life with a bang. A natural athlete and full of energy, he spent his high school years working out and playing football, enjoying the accolades and adrenaline rush of being the team hero. College, on the other hand, was a bit of a blur. Eli would say he minored in business and history and majored in sports and fun.

After graduation, he started working at an accounting firm. The money was good, but for Eli the job was mind-numbing. His boredom grew, and any sense of adventure or accomplishment shriveled to insignificance in the daily drudgery of crunching numbers.

It was also a desk job, and Eli soon found himself out of shape, tired, and without much motivation to get off the couch after work. Within two years, this general malaise grew into full-blown depression. By the time he called in to the New Life radio show asking for help, his despair was so deep it made him want to give up on life. He knew something had to change, but what?

Then there's Jesse, a classic Renaissance man who found his meaning and purpose in whatever creative or intellectual endeavor he pursued. Even as a kid, he loved music, art, writing poetry, and reading literary fiction. His dad, a sports enthusiast and sometimes angry alcoholic, was open about his disappointment with Jesse's bookishness and lack of interest in athletics.

When Jesse was eighteen, he left his small Southern town for New York City, where he found work as an assistant copy-editor at a trendy magazine. In time, he met and married Jen, a practical thinker and upbeat young woman who balanced out the cerebral, angsty, artsy, sometimes melancholy parts of his personality. Despite their differences, they shared a love of nature. Walks in Central Park became part of their daily routine. They both had a quirky sense of humor and loved going to local theater productions.

But even though Jen was cheerful and fun to be with, she didn't enjoy philosophy, wasn't a reader, and didn't ponder the meaning of life the way Jesse did. Sometimes he wished Jen could be the kind of companion who enjoyed discussions of ideas, theories, and beliefs. For the most part, though, he was left to find these kinds of fulfilling interactions at work.

Over time, Jesse formed a close friendship with Stella, one of the bookish, thoughtful women in the office. When he conversed with Stella about what he had been reading or contemplating, he felt alive. He came to see me (Dave) when he realized he was falling for Stella in ways that worried him. He loved Jen, but his inability to connect with her in deeper, intellectual conversations negatively affected his feelings of closeness to her. Stella seemed to fill an empty spot in his life. Was he in love with her?

Finally there's Ryan, a successful corporate salesman who accepted an early retirement package when his company downsized to stay afloat. His kids were grown and gone, and all four of his grandkids were in high school. During his first year of retirement, Ryan and his wife traveled the country, and he also played lots of golf.

But without his career, Ryan felt emotionally adrift. Something was missing. His job had kept him busy enough that he'd never taken the time to ask many questions about God, his own place in the universe, or his purpose. He'd never made time for friendships with other men during the years of raising kids and focusing on paying the bills and climbing the corporate ladder. At age fifty-eight, he realized he might have only fifteen or twenty years left to live. He wanted those years to be meaningful. He wanted the rest of his life to count.

Though these men were at different crossroads, and though they were at different ages and stages of life, they shared one thing in common: They had not yet fully tapped into the soul of the hero inside themselves. "Locate and nourish your inner hero in healthy ways, and you'll begin to feel alive again," we promised them.

Through a series of questions and lessons, healthy risks, and new discoveries and adventures (the very things we'll look at in this book), these men became reenergized. With fresh insights into their place in God's heart and their purpose in the world, their lives began to change in profound and beneficial ways. They became more secure, more at ease with God and others, and more confident in their identity and mission.

Eli realized that his true calling involved helping others, belonging to some sort of team, and challenging himself physically. With these new insights, he made a radical change in his career path and became a firefighter. As he discovered a vocation that brought him meaning and adventure, along with the joy of constantly learning new skills, he noticed an interesting change in his perspective.

After an exhausting but satisfying day on the scene of a huge apartment fire, Eli realized he *liked* the man he was becoming. He felt God's pleasure as he helped others out of danger. The first time he saved a child from a burning building and delivered her unharmed to her frantic and grateful mother was the closest Eli had ever felt to being Superman, his childhood hero. He felt as if he'd gone from being a boy adrift in the world to a real man on a mission. He woke up every morning grateful to God for a chance to change people's lives and bring a little of heaven's caring love to earth.

In short, Eli found the soul of a hero—and realized it had already been inside him.

Jesse discovered, over time and in counseling, that he was dealing with some unresolved father wounds. He found that his hunger for deeper conversations about life and his longing for philosophical and spiritual interaction could be met through healthy male mentors and a close fellowship of friends. He joined a group of aspiring writers, well-read thinkers, and spiritually curious men who met on Saturday mornings for coffee and conversation. They shared from whatever they were reading and writing, and they pondered the deeper questions of life together.

This new group met several needs in Jesse's life. The leader was an older man who gave Jesse the kind of fatherly affirmation he'd longed for as a boy. The other men became brothers in their mutual search for meaning and creative ways to use their writing gifts. He no longer felt like such an odd duck in the world of men.

As Jesse began to get in touch with the creative inner hero in his soul, he found the courage to start writing a novel, an epic fantasy full of heroes and villains and overcoming danger. Every time he sat down to write, he felt like he was diving into an adventure, and he could sense God's pleasure in the creative process. He also found a greater appreciation for Jen's qualities of lightness, fun, and enjoyment of nature, realizing that these things provided a healthy balance to his introspective writing process. He needed her to pull him out of his own head and encourage him to get some fresh air, laughter, and fun. Their communication improved as they began to value the differences each one brought to their marriage and find healthy ways to nurture their varied interests. As Jesse tapped into the soul of a hero within himself, he discovered the pathway to a much happier, healthier, and more meaningful life.

And Ryan? Well, Ryan took stock of his life and began spending time with a spiritual director and life coach, who helped him in his search for meaning. Through conversation, thought, and prayer, Ryan was able to define what he wanted to do with the remaining years of his life: prioritize his time so he could put energy and focus into those things that would help him finish well and leave a lasting legacy.

One day Ryan had an idea. The country was in the early days of the COVID-19 pandemic, and he wanted to do something to make a difference. He shared his idea with his wife, and she was immediately on board. They wanted to inspire and encourage the men and women who were stepping up to take care of those who were extremely ill from the virus. The idea was to mobilize restauranteurs, who had been forced to shut down their in-house dining, to prepare meals for health care workers and first responders, thus keeping their kitchens open and their workforce employed.

Immediately Ryan set out to raise $2 million, calling business associates from his former career and the heads of several foundations. While he raised the money, his wife contacted the eating establishments and organized them to provide breakfasts, lunches, or dinners. She also gathered a volunteer team to pick up the food in donated rental trucks and deliver it to local hospitals, firehouses, and police stations.

Four phone calls were all it took for Ryan to raise the necessary funds. Then he helped his wife roll out the entire operation in five days. It was a total win for everyone. One heroic act begets another, and it wasn't long before Ryan's idea began to spread and inspire more people to start heroic movements of care and compassion during a time of great anxiety for so many.

As Ryan tapped into the soul of a hero within himself, he

was well on his way to leaving a legacy of caring and love that would outlast his life in many positive ways.

A Rat's Tale: Enrich Your Life, and Your Problems Will Shrink

Though we have much in common as men, we each have a unique calling as well. After we understand our place in God's eyes, our individual mission, and a few core truths about the masculine soul (which we will discuss in later chapters), and then begin to implement these insights, a whole host of troubling issues will diminish or simply disappear. Discouragement will give way to a sense of adventure; fatigue will yield to an excitement to get the day started; and temptations and addictions may seem to lose their appeal. We've seen it time and again: When men discover their true heroic soul, they begin to grow and give in healthy ways. Men who have been searching for purpose and direction find themselves energized and focused. Others, who feared their best years were behind them, find a second wind that helps them live every remaining day filled with joy and enthusiasm.

Dave and I have both found our career calling—and feel God's pleasure in our lives—as we work in the areas of counseling, recovery, and speaking God's truth. I do this mostly through hosting a daily radio call-in show (*New Life Live!*); serving as the teaching pastor of Northview Church in Carmel, Indiana; speaking in various venues; producing specialty Bibles; and writing books. I find all these avenues for outreach endlessly and enormously meaningful and exciting.

Dave has also authored many helpful books and has decades of experience in one-on-one counseling. We have written several books together, shared speaking platforms, and often work in the radio booth together. Though we have several passions in common, perhaps the most obvious one is our heart for men who are trapped in destructive habits, dependencies, and addictions. We love seeing "the captives set free."[1]

In our years of ministering to men who are facing the typical male problems of addiction, temptation, aimlessness, and wounding, we have observed a remarkable truth: When we are able to help a man find his inner heroic soul, many of his troubling issues naturally start to fall away. Frankly, it makes our counseling job much easier and more enjoyable. Rather than focusing on the symptomatic problems, we focus on helping each man get in touch with his heroic heart and purpose and then nourish those things. Our job is to point the way, to call men to a higher path and a greater adventure—one that won't give them a headache in the morning, land them in jail, ruin their marriages, or worse.

This idea—of increasing the conditions needed for mental and spiritual health so that unhelpful habits or sabotaging tendencies fade—is not original with us; but in our opinion, it is often underutilized.

Our interest in the concept of emotional healing was piqued by an experiment conducted with rats. A team of research scientists discovered that amazing things happened when lab rats that were hopelessly addicted to a mood-altering drug were taken out of their small, boring cages and put into large, super-enriched environments.[2] The new surroundings were spacious and filled with a variety of great rat-sized exercise equipment, rodent-pleasing food, and spaces to run and explore with plenty of fun-loving rat friends. It was a rat's dream house. To the surprise of the researchers, once placed in "Rat Park," the previously addicted rats chose to drink pure water over the drug-laced liquid. In other words, their real life had become more exciting, fun, and rewarding than a drug. And they didn't want to miss out by being numbed up or zoned out on chemicals. There was no need for an altered state when real life was this enjoyable; and at least in this experiment, the addiction that had once ruled their lives simply dropped away.

We should add here that breaking an addiction is more complicated than simply creating a happy, active, interesting environment. But environment—especially one that is rich in meaningful connections with others—is a huge and often overlooked factor in cultivating mental health and avoiding dangerous temptations. Any good treatment program involves helping an addict create a hope-filled, purposeful, and fun vision of the future, one that will help override the pull back into the addiction cycle.

More often than not, Dave and I have seen that when we motivate men to create the conditions that call out their best selves, their souls begin to flourish, and addictions, sins, bad habits, negativity, and depression tend to lessen. This usually means connecting to their heroic soul and creating conditions to nourish their heart, mind, body, and spirit. When a man connects with the hero in his own heart, he becomes more giving, caring, fun, and optimistic—qualities that are attractive to others. His social connections grow. His spirit thrives. His mood brightens. A man who is fully alive is a joy to behold. As Howard Thurman, the renowned African American scholar and theologian, said, "Don't ask yourself what the world needs. Ask yourself what makes you come alive, and go do that, because what this world needs is people who have come alive."[3] The world needs men who have come alive to their worth, their purpose, and their passion.

I wonder where you are on your life's journey as you read this page. Perhaps you are experiencing a major crisis in midlife and feel that you need an overhaul. Maybe you're basically happy and balanced but you'd like to have more purpose, more meaning, and experience more joy and more peace. Maybe you'd like a little more *superpower* in your daily life, and you're looking for the skills to keep harmful temptations and bad habits at bay while increasing your connection with family and friends.

You know the old saying, "Bloom where you're planted"? In this book, we'll explore a slight alternative to this classic advice: "Plant yourself where you can bloom best." We often counsel men in crisis or recovery to proactively and purposefully create an environment where their heroic masculine soul—their best God-created self—can most easily and naturally stretch, grow, and blossom.

The details of your enriched environment will vary from that of other men. But as you incorporate the seven "heroic secrets," which we'll explain in the following chapters, you will learn how to empty yourself and begin as a child; embrace your true identity in the eyes of God; find mentors and brothers to journey with you; discover your earthly purpose; learn how to love and respect a woman's heart; and win the war within by mastering your mind. Over time, and with practice, the unique environment you develop (both internal and external) will take you from where you are to where you want to be in life. Desire and determination are all you need to practice these skills until they become a natural part of your daily life. It's simply a matter of priority and commitment.

You may have heard the following short metaphorical tale before. It's an old story, but it contains a profound truth and is worth repeating here.

A beloved and respected old man was asked by a young buck one day, "How do you always manage to respond so wisely and kindly? Why is your life so brave and good?"

The old man said, "Ah, my son, it didn't happen naturally. There is always a black dog and a white dog fighting within me. One urges me to act badly;

the other to rise above and do the good thing, the right thing."

"Which dog wins?" the young man asked.

"The one that I feed the most," the old man answered with a wink.

The Soul of a Hero is about feeding the good dog with regular nourishment. As you do so, the bad dog gets weaker and the good dog grows stronger.

To put it another way, rather than spending a lot of time shouting at the darkness (warning men not to behave badly), we've found it far more effective to light a candle (to point men toward their unique hero's journey). If you turn a man's face toward the sun, show him what he is capable of becoming, and encourage his masculine soul to shine, he will find he doesn't have nearly as much idle time to get into trouble or the desire to drift into the dark places. He'll be too busy loving his real, awesome, amazing life. This is what Jesus meant when he promised to give us "a rich and satisfying life."[4] Good soul nourishment, an enriched environment, wisdom skills, and a heart of service can work miracles in a man who has lost his masculine mojo or who simply wants to be the best he can be.

Myths versus True Heroes

Our deepest desire in writing this book is for you to become the hero of your own story. But what does that really mean?

Are we talking about becoming like Heracles, the mythological hero from ancient Greece who was known for his courage, strength, ingenuity, and physical endurance—but was notably lacking in character? Or like one of the popular Marvel or DC superheroes who disguises his true identity? The popularity of superhero movies in our day suggests that many people—men and women alike—are longing for something more than what they find in their own lives. But who could measure up to the exploits of these mythical heroes? No one! Like so many other male myths, these make-believe heroes leave us feeling weak and inferior, unable to live up to an impossible standard.

Though many people equate heroism with power, strength, ingenuity, and maybe a hint of mystery, true biblical heroism has more to do with faithfulness, authenticity, loyalty, and commitment than with physical ability or bicep girth.

Think of the days of Noah, when no one could imagine floodwaters erupting from the earth and a mighty deluge of rain pouring down from the sky.[5] God told Noah to build a gigantic boat so that he, his family, and two of every kind of creature could be saved from some crazy, never-before-seen flood that was coming. But God didn't include a CAD program and a laptop with his instructions, and it took Noah 120 years of hard work to build the ark—amid a torrent of ridicule from his neighbors.

Twice the Bible mentions that Noah accomplished everything God asked him to do.[6] By his decades-long obedience, he became a hero to his family, to God, and to all the generations that would follow him. By choosing to believe God's word to him over what he saw and heard, Noah became a hero of faith.

Even the most impressive superhero from a comic book or blockbuster movie can't hold a candle to Moses, another true biblical hero. He did not cower in fear, even when Pharaoh kept refusing to let God's people go despite falling victim to numerous plagues, including the death of his firstborn son. No, Moses kept coming back to face the stubborn monarch until Pharaoh finally relented.

Neither did Moses cower later on at the Red Sea. He marched everyone right through the parted waters and then into the wilderness. Moses led the Israelites out of captivity and toward the Promised Land, day after day. Even though the Israelites often veered away from God, Moses never abandoned them. He delivered his people to the front door of the Promised Land.

Moses was a hero of persistence, refusing to give up and meeting Pharaoh's pride and the waywardness of the Israelites with God-given determination.

King David's courage was evident even when he was a young boy spending his days minding sheep, writing psalms, and playing a harp in the wilderness. In those days, the giant Goliath was known for his incredible strength, and he was the hero of his tribe. But being a hero to the wrong crowd is not heroism at all. When Goliath terrorized the people of Israel, no man was brave enough to fight him. So David, who was too small to wear King Saul's armor, became the courageous hero who put a stop to Goliath's terrorism and taunting.

David had two things going for him. First, he had courage that was fueled and directed by an awesome God. All those years of communing with God in nature, writing psalms of praise, and tending sheep had made David spiritually secure and unafraid. In addition, after years of driving away predators from the flock, David knew how to handle a slingshot, which was a perfect weapon against a much larger foe.

David was a hero of courage. His physical skill and deep trust in God helped to secure a victory for his people against seemingly insurmountable odds.

In the New Testament, the apostles were ordinary men who lived for Jesus, serving him and spreading his Word, even when confronted with cruel treatment, ridicule, and death. They weren't perfect, but they were persistent and wholehearted in their heroic dedication to Christ.

Heroes are made by the paths they choose,
not the powers they are graced with.

BRODI ASHTON, *EVERNEATH*

In our day, the world longs for such examples of faith, persistence, and courage. WE NEED HEROES! More precisely, we need every man to be a hero—including *you*. We believe God brought you to this book for a reason. You have a destiny, designed by God, to pursue a heroic calling. Your journey may not look like any other man's, but if you will implement the seven heroic truths we discuss in the coming pages, you will not regret it. You will be well on your way to living the abundant life that God has promised. We believe that every man, beginning in childhood, dreams of becoming a hero in some way. But not every man is willing to do what it takes to answer God's higher calling.

Are you ready to live an extraordinary life? A life of true biblical heroism? We hope and pray that you are.

If you are willing, let us show you the way to the soul of a hero.

COME EMPTY

Heroic Secret #1: Begin as a Child

Courage, child:
we are all between the paws
of the true Aslan.

C. S. LEWIS, *THE LAST BATTLE*

You may not feel as if you have the raw materials for heroism. But let us assure you, you have everything you need—which is to say . . . *nothing*. Believe it or not, the emptier you feel and the more you realize how much you don't know, the less there will be for you to unlearn when you answer the call of the Master Teacher. Just come as you are, bringing only your honest self, and you will be well equipped.

Come as You Are

Have you ever thought about the differences between a women's retreat and a men's campout? The women assign a planning committee months in advance and schedule all kinds of activities—from crafts to skits to music to games. They arrange for real meals with vegetables, appetizers, and fancy cupcakes. They also have a decorating committee so the facility will be done up as pretty as a fancy boutique hotel. They make cute little name tags. They have breakout sessions and discussion leaders, as well as artsy pamphlets that feature the full agenda and the speakers' bios. It's enough to make a guy's head spin.

Men, on the other hand, start planning the camping weekend the night before it begins. They call a hunting buddy and ask him to bring any elk or deer meat he has in the freezer. Appetizers are bags of chips and packages of store-bought cookies. A complete dinner for a man is Doritos, Oreos, and a venison steak. That's it. Breakfast is scrambled eggs by the dozen and pounds of fried bacon. Maybe some pancakes if the guys are feeling ambitious.

Whatever clothes and toiletries men need on a campout should fit in a gallon-size ziplock. Done. It's a total come-as-you-are, no-fluff, no-bother affair.

Some guys will bring their guitars. Others will have their Bibles and share a few verses. Somebody else will pray. Another will bring horseshoes.

Men don't like to talk a lot, so there are no planned discussion groups. No need for an itinerary. It just unfolds and happens. That's how most men roll when you let them do what they really want to do.

In a dress-to-impress, get 'er done world, most men are starving for a no-frills campout. Can you imagine joining a group of laid-back, welcoming buddies who have no expectations for what you should say or do or wear or be? Without any need to impress anyone? Leave behind that stuff you've been hauling around that's weighing you down and come out to the piney woods. Breathe some mountain air. You are welcome and wanted, no résumé required. The bacon's frying and the coffee is percolating. Grab a plate and mug, pull up a chair or a log around the warm fire, and put your feet up. You belong.

Can you feel it? That feeling of "Ahhhh . . . this is good." That feeling of coming home to yourself, surrounded by others who are doing the same thing.

Throughout the Gospels, Jesus, the Master Teacher, invites us to come.

Just come.

That's where we want to begin this book—with an invitation to just show up.

Come empty-handed. Come like a kid on a campout. Bring nothing but yourself and a deep sigh of relief.

Plenty of Nothin'

"Steve, I got nothin'," men will tell me.

And I reply, "Awesome. Plenty of nothin' is exactly what you need to start again."

In a spirit of shared brokenness, I offer an example of a time when I had to admit I had nothing.

Misty and I had been married for only a few years, but the thrill was gone, to say the least. We were feeling low, helpless, and stuck. It was a place neither one of us thought was possible when we married with such hopes and dreams and self-confidence—not to mention years of collective knowledge about relationships. But we'd hit the proverbial wall as a couple, and neither of us was able to understand or hear the other. So we did what I have advised thousands of couples to do during my years of ministry: We went to see a marriage counselor together.

Misty gave her perspective and revealed that she felt nothing for me. I knew it was true, but it was extremely piercing to hear her say it out loud to another person. It brought the full weight of the sickness in our marriage right into my lap. Then I told the counselor that I had also reached a point where I felt nothing. Not even anger. No feelings at all.

The counselor let us know that she heard us and understood how painful it must be (because that's what counselors do). Then she surprised us by saying, "It seems you both have something very powerful in common: You both feel nothing for each other. So let's start there. Let's start with common ground."

And that's what we did, even though what we felt for each other was *nothing*. Whether the counselor knew it, I don't know—but *we* knew that God not only meets us at the bottom of life but is also a specialist at making something out of nothing.

When the counselor asked us to start at zero again, we had to unlearn some bad habits and assumptions we had brought into our marriage. She encouraged us to become more curious, childlike, and humble, willing to learn with fresh eyes and an open mind about the unique person we had married. As it turned out, we were more complex than any how-to book we'd read or marriage class we'd taken had given us credit for.

We didn't know it then, but we were entering a master's-level training course, led by a wise mentor, on how to love the actual *us*—not the image of the perfect couple we had assumed we would be, but the honest, actual, real people we were. To earn a master's in "each other," and to do it well, we had to come empty—stripped of our pride, assumptions, expectations, and habitual ways of handling issues—so that we could be filled back up with wisdom and love based on the reality of who we really were. We had to create a *new* marriage in which we could both be our best selves and flourish together. We also had to humble ourselves before God, admitting we were stuck and numb and without vision. We asked God to refill us with his love and his Spirit and show us the way to real connection.

Allow me to fast-forward the story to tell you that he did that and more![1] To our surprise and everlasting gratitude, God answered our empty-handed prayers and filled us up with true love and passion that was based on deeply listening to, understanding, and appreciating each other. We brought what we could to him—our tired and discouraged selves. He took that offering and multiplied it as we practiced the Master's lessons of love. Our thankfulness for God's work in our marriage still overflows.

Spiritual Multiplication

As I was writing this chapter, I began to think of all the metaphors Jesus used about bringing him something empty or very small (like a mustard seed) so that he can do the filling up, the growing, and the multiplying for us—supernaturally. Turns out his life and teaching were full of such examples.

There was the time he asked to borrow a boat from Simon, a scruffy fisherman, and used it as a floating pulpit to preach to the crowd that had gathered on the beach. Afterward he told the surprised fisherman to row out deeper and cast his nets. The men in the boat probably laughed at him because they had been fishing all night and had caught *nothing*. Nada. Nichts. The nets were so empty that not even a minnow could be found. But because they had just heard him preach, and because it was Jesus, the ultimate Master Teacher, who had asked for their cooperation, Simon decided to humor him and obey his suggestion. They soon found their nets so full they had to call another boat of friends over to help them drag in the abundant catch.[2]

Soon after the men had pulled in their haul of fish, Jesus gave them a real mission, one with eternal meaning: "Follow me," he said, "and I will show you how to fish for people!"[3] Four fishermen left their nets and boats that day and started the Master's training course in how to reel in people with Good News from God. They just walked off down the dusty road, a bunch of guys who smelled like fish, with nothing but their robes and sandals, following a teacher who promised miracles and meaning. They didn't know it then, but together this motley crew would change the world—bringing hope and meaning and eternal life to multitudes of people. And it all started with an empty net.

Remember how Jesus multiplied two measly fish and five little loaves of bread into a miracle feast for five thousand hungry men? He wasn't satisfied with giving everyone just enough. He turned that little meal into such abundance that there were twelve basketfuls of food left over—a doggie bag for each disciple to enjoy later.[4]

Give Jesus whatever you have and let him bless it; then stand back and watch for the overflow.

The disciples also saw Jesus ask that six stone water jars, each capable of holding 20 to 30 gallons of water for ceremonial washing, be filled with water. The result was 120 to 180 gallons of the finest wine. Talk about abundance![5]

Every empty thing that Jesus fills he seems to fill to overflowing, beyond what is needed. Truth be told, God seems to enjoy showing what he can do with little or nothing.

The first step on the journey to uncovering your heroic masculine soul is simple: Start humbly and bring what you've got—even if it's a whole lot of nothing. God can work with that. In fact, his power is perfected in our weakness.[6] A self-reliant, biased-for-action know-it-all doesn't have enough room in his heart for God's best surprises. But the man who holds out his empty bowl and asks God to fill it—as the Lord sees fit—is the one who will discover the true meaning of abundance, purpose, and significance.

A Beginner's Mindset

In most of the great stories of men-turned-heroes, there is a point where they must let go of all their pride and previous knowledge, allowing themselves to start over with a child's mind and be mentored in the master's ways. Jedi knights had to let go of their own logic and learn the way of the Force. When Doctor Strange, a brilliant surgeon, lost the use of his hands, he had to humble himself, let go of his arrogance, learn a mystical new way of seeing, and harness a new kind of power to help the world. Almost every superhero movie shows the point at which a mortal man realizes he possesses a power that must be harnessed, trained, and used for a cause greater than himself. But in order to do that, he must let go of his former way of doing things to make room for new wisdom. Often a wise mentor helps in the process. Think of Obi-Wan Kenobi and Yoda in *Star Wars*; Mr. Miyagi in *The Karate Kid*; Aslan in The Chronicles of Narnia; Gandalf in The Lord of the Rings; and Dr. Sean Maguire in *Good Will Hunting*. Even Winnie-the-Pooh has a wise mentor in Christopher Robin. Typically the mentor begins by encouraging his student to become a beginner, to drop old ways of thinking at the door of the classroom.

The hero's saga begins with an emptying of pride; the unlearning of old, habitual ways of thinking; and yielding to the master, who knows a better and higher way. In his teaching parables (brief stories with a point), Jesus was forever saying, "You have heard it said . . . but I tell you . . ." In other words, "Common wisdom says thus-and-so, but I will teach you a higher way of viewing and doing things."

The journey to uncovering your heroic soul begins with embracing a childlike (not childish) mind and heart—letting go of old and unhelpful thought loops—and opening yourself up to God's higher way—the Kingdom way of doing things.

One of the most profound and humbling master life lessons that I (Dave) had to learn was when my middle son started using heroin at the age of eighteen. Back in the 1980s, addiction training wasn't part of regular doctoral counseling programs. My wife and I had no idea that the issue of addiction was unique and complex, and that "doing what felt natural" as a parent and therapist wasn't going to cut it. We sent our son to a regular counselor, who tried traditional therapies with him, and it was a complete failure. I also set up a couple of situations that I just *knew* would work—where God would do a miracle and my son would give up drugs.

Those, too, failed miserably.

Finally my wife and I dropped what we thought we knew and came to God like two confused kids in need of guidance. We gave up trying to save our son by our own wits and started praying. We settled in for a long wait as we gave our son to God and trusted him to work in our son's life in any way he wanted.

During this time, I was teaching Sunday school. One Saturday evening, our son disappeared with the car and didn't come home—and we had no idea where he was. We had been through enough drama by then to know that he was most likely on a run—a drug binge—and oblivious to our worries and concerns.

Tired, discouraged, and in a lot of emotional pain, I had nothing left in me to prepare a Sunday school lesson. And because I was a psychologist and a Bible teacher, I thought if I told the class what my family was going through, they would judge us as failures and maybe even walk out. But I was too broken to care.

On that pivotal Sunday morning, I showed up empty

and shared what was happening. To my surprise, the class responded with empathy, understanding, and tremendous emotional support. They undergirded us with prayer. We were no longer alone. What a huge relief! Because I had come to class empty of wisdom, with no lesson, offering only honesty, God was able to move in tremendously healing ways. Little did I know it was right where he had wanted me all along.

Next we gave up everything we thought we knew about parenting—things we'd learned from our experience and our background in counseling—and we joined a group where we listened to addicts in recovery. This, too, was hard on my ego. As a therapist, I was used to *leading* groups. But now I was just another frightened dad in need of help—which was also exactly where God wanted me.

When I introduced myself at one of the initial meetings by saying, "I'm here because my son has an addiction problem," one of the young recovering addicts just about came out of his chair.

"Ha!" he said. "That's what my dad used say. But he found out it was *him* who had the problem!"

I was taken aback, but as I got to know that young man, it turned out he was right. My wife and I soon learned that addiction was in large part a family issue, and we learned to take responsibility for our part in our son's emotional pain. But we also learned that loving an addict means throwing away a lot of what comes naturally to parents. We had to relearn how to love our son and establish boundaries. To stop rescuing him when he was arrested. To set limits. None of this was easy. In fact, much of it was difficult and unnatural and painful. But our new mentors—recovering addicts and their parents—helped us learn new, healthier ways of coping and caring for both ourselves and our son.

It took ten often harrowing, roller-coaster years. But our son has now been free of addiction for thirty years. We got him back. And I can tell you with 100 percent certainty that it was nothing we can take credit for. It was all God. We came broken. We came empty. We gave the whole mess of our son's addiction and our parenting mistakes to God. When we were at the point of humility—realizing we had *nothin'*—the right mentors appeared with fresh lessons for us. Our best teachers were young, outspoken, recovering addicts in holey jeans and ragged T-shirts. You never know what your best mentors may look like!

I know there may be parents reading this who feel they have forever lost a child to drugs, to the street. My heart goes out to you. I wish I could jump out of this book and hug you personally and pray for you. In fact, over the past few decades, I have been able to minister to parents of prodigals who are in deep pain—not as a know-it-all counselor, but as a fellow pilgrim who has traveled the long, chaotic, painful road and who has learned healthy ways to cope from unlikely teachers in the trenches.

It happened only because I gave up plotting and trying. I came empty and honest to people who loved our family and prayed for us, and to fellow pilgrims who put their arms around us and taught us new and better ways through the long, unknown journey ahead. It didn't feel like much of an adventure, but looking back on it, I see that being a parent of an addict is an adventure like no other. It's often like being in a movie where the hero has to duck in and out of near disaster, where crisis comes out of the blue, where monsters lurk and horrible pits of despair must be crossed. There are mountaintop moments of hope, often followed by dizzying drops into discouragement. There is also a heightened awareness that without God and prayer and fellow pilgrims, you have no chance of making it through alive and mostly sane. If that isn't an adventure, I don't know what is.

Relying on God has to begin all over again
every day as if nothing had yet been done.

C. S. LEWIS, *THE COLLECTED LETTERS OF C. S. LEWIS*

The late Gary Smalley was a prolific writer, a hilarious speaker, and a good friend. He said that when problems came along, he learned to say, "Whoopee! God is about to teach me something new!" Wouldn't it be great if, when a problem came into your path, you immediately took a childlike approach and came eager and empty-handed to your Master Teacher, ready to learn the new lessons he has for you?

Give It All to Jesus

At the height of his earthly ministry, Jesus prayed an interesting prayer. After prophesying sorrow for those who had witnessed "so many of his miracles [but] hadn't repented of their sins and turned to God,"[7] he prays, "O Father, Lord of heaven and earth, thank you for hiding these things from those who think themselves wise and clever, and for revealing them to the childlike. Yes, Father, it pleased you to do it this way!"[8]

A few verses later, he offers an invitation: "Come to me, all of you who are weary and carry heavy burdens, and I will give you rest."[9]

In this passage, Jesus sounds like more than just a wise teacher. He was obviously feeling parental and fatherly toward the twelve men he had mentored and loved. When we say, "Come to me" to someone who looks weary and burdened, what are we inviting him or her to do? We want them to come into our arms, where we can give a good old bear hug.

This same theme appears again in Matthew 19, when Jesus tells his disciples, "Let the children come to me. Don't stop them! For the Kingdom of Heaven belongs to those who are like these children."[10] Something about our coming with a childlike spirit—open, willing, without pretense, without anything to offer—pleases the heart of God.

When we are world-weary and beaten down, it takes a lot of affirmation and assurance to get us back on our feet. Especially when we have deeply disappointed ourselves and others and need the kind of forgiveness we can't earn—the kind of forgiveness that can only be called grace or mercy.

If you've ever read *The Lion, the Witch and the Wardrobe*, by C. S. Lewis, you will remember the selfishness of the youngest brother, Edmund. Because of his obsessive desire for Turkish Delight, he sells out his siblings to the rule and realm of the wicked White Witch. All manner of trouble, mischief, and tragedy ensue. At Edmund's lowest point, as he's about to be killed by evil forces, Aslan, the great lion and Christ figure in the story, sends a rescue party to save him.

Lewis then describes a long, private conversation between Edmund and Aslan as they walk together through a field: "There is no need to tell you (and no one ever heard) what Aslan was saying, but it was a conversation which Edmund never forgot."[11]

By forgoing his typical use of detail and dialogue here, Lewis conveys that what transpires between Edmund and Aslan is holy and private. Even the reader cannot venture into that holy of holies, that private moment of forgiveness, assurance, redemption, and validation.

Edmund comes back from his ordeal a changed boy. Humbled. Restored. Wiser. Aslan will hear no more of Edmund's past mistakes and wrong choices, nor will he allow anyone else to speak of them. Most heroes must go through some kind of failure or brokenness on their journeys, and that part of Edmund's heroic coming-of-age is now over. Yet it reflects a profound recognition of our own need to be rescued and forgiven. It knocks the rough edges of pride from our spirit.

Edmund is later knighted in Aslan's presence and goes on to become a wise ruling prince of Narnia, but in truth, Edmund's identity has always been that of a royal hero. He may have looked like a boy who would sell out his family for a bite of Turkish Delight, but Aslan saw through this false self. And when Edmund was exhausted of all desire to hide and pretend, when he had nothing to say or offer, when he realized he could not save himself, Aslan quickly, thoroughly, and deeply forgave him and reminded him of the hero he was destined to be in the kingdom of Narnia.

It takes some of us boy-men a while—and many mistakes with our own forms of Turkish Delight—to finally come to Aslan empty-handed. But rest assured, when we are ready to arrive in Aslan's presence with a whole lot of nothin' to offer him, we will open ourselves up to untold riches—hearts overflowing with grace and gratitude, along with a new identity and a fresh mission.

No matter how old you are or where you are in life, it is never too late to become the hero of the story God is writing for you.

Just start as a child.

Come empty into God's strong and fatherly arms.

Jesus said, "Let the children come to me. Don't stop them! For the Kingdom of Heaven belongs to those who are like these children."

MATTHEW 19:14

YOUR TRUE IDENTITY

Heroic Secret #2: You Are Who God Says You Are

*Define yourself radically as one beloved by God; God's love
for you and his choice of you constitute your worth. Accept that,
and let it become the most important thing in your life.*

JOHN EAGAN, *A TRAVELER TOWARD THE DAWN*

Lately it seems as if every time I (Steve) am listening to the radio in my car, a commercial comes on that I can't ignore. The speaker is a guy who worked with me in the early days of New Life. Back then, he used to warn me that insurance companies wouldn't cover long-term psychiatric care much longer—implying that if I needed it, the sooner I checked myself in, the better. Funny guy. Now he's on the radio, warning me to protect myself and all my assets from identity theft. The commercials say it happens all the time, and the end result, if you're not protected by their product, may be the loss of everything you own.

Identity theft is nothing new. For us men, it has been happening ever since Adam choked on an apple instead of being the hero he could and should have been for the woman he loved. He lost his mojo, and instead of steering Eve away from Satan's trap, he fell into it as well. As a result, they both lost their way, lost Eden, and lost much, much more.

Why did Adam and Eve lose their way—and their minds? Why couldn't they do two simple things: avoid eating the forbidden fruit and watch out for snakes?

Because they were not 100 percent certain of their identity. They allowed it to be stolen by the trickster in the Garden. They forgot for a moment who they really were: beloved children of God, the Creator of everything. In fact, they were such intimate friends with God that they would walk with him in the Garden in the cool of the day, enjoying each other's company, shooting the breeze. But for whatever reason, momentarily detached from the memory of their Maker and Mentor, they succumbed to the lure of a conniving snake who held out false promises of power.[1] I refuse to point the finger at Adam, though, because I know I would have done the exact same thing. And you would have too.

Of Frogs and Men

A common theme in many well-known stories, both in the Bible and elsewhere, is men who have lost sight of their true identity. Since time began, people have told different versions of the fallen-hero tale that begins with someone exchanging his birthright for a mess of porridge or a tasty piece of fruit from a forbidden tree. Or for magic beans. Or Turkish Delight. But temptation only tempts us when we forget about who we are and everything we already have—when we act like frogs croaking in a pond instead of embracing our true identity as princes in a Kingdom that calls us to a higher mission.

Thankfully, God is creative. He uses all kinds of things—all manner of people and places and happenings and stories and words and more—to break the spell of false beliefs and restore us to our true identity and get us back to the hero's journey.

For most men, a huge part of their identity comes from a sense of belonging to a family or group of people who love, accept, and believe in them. I (Dave) grew up with an emotionally absent and sometimes abusive father. I also have three sons of my own, so perhaps that's why one of my favorite TV shows is *Blue Bloods*, the story of a close-knit Irish Catholic family that includes three generations of police officers and an assistant district attorney. The dad, Frank Reagan (played by Tom Selleck), is the current New York City police commissioner. Frank's father, Henry, is a former police commissioner and police officer. Now retired and a widower, Henry makes sure that every member of the family shows up and sits down for their weekly Sunday family dinner, no matter what conflicts have come up during the week. (And there are plenty.)

I'm fascinated by the premise of the show: four generations of strong, independent, flawed men (and women and teens) who often disagree and argue but, at the end of the week, sit around the family table, say grace, and remember that they belong to each other, to God, and to the high calling of doing something good in the world. Sometimes that includes admitting they were wrong and apologizing—which is never easy for this proud bunch. But they do it because their highest identity is that they are Reagans. They belong to each other. They are family—and it's a good, strong, loving, and supportive clan.

In one episode, after a series of heartbreaking events, Frank tells everyone at the table, just before the family says the blessing over Sunday dinner, "When we have everyone we love, we have everything. And for that we should be grateful. And no matter the hardship or the loss, this family does not stand down. Ever."[2]

Those words always get to me.

I wonder how many men have watched *Blue Bloods* and can only imagine what it would be like to belong to such a family, where you are always welcome at the dinner table, equal in importance to everyone else, and surrounded by that comforting, warm, safe emotion of belonging—even if you are temporarily angry or frustrated or have really messed up. You know who you are: a Reagan. With all the glory and all the flaws that go with the family name, you know your identity, and you're proud of it.

Well, here's a sneak preview of your true identity. Are you ready for this? You are an adopted son of God, which is even better than being a Reagan. You are a deeply loved child of the Most High, with all the rights and privileges that go along with belonging to his family. You are also a member of "a chosen people, a royal priesthood, a holy nation, God's special possession, that you may declare the praises of him who called you out of darkness into his wonderful light."[3] You belong to this family; you are a son of the Creator, with a mission and a purpose on earth. Yep, flaws and all, mistakes and all. And that's just for starters.

Warrior in Hiding

A friend and colleague of ours, a fellow writer, recently shared a story that we thought was a classic example of remembering our true identities when we are disoriented by the slings and arrows of life. At the time, our friend was a primary school teacher with a bad case of poison ivy. The man in this story was actually a frightened seven-year-old boy. Here is what our friend wrote:

One summer I drove myself to a minor emergency clinic, desperate for relief from a killer case of poison ivy I'd somehow contracted. I wanted to end my misery before hitting the sandy beaches of Florida for a week of vacation. Upon arrival, I was led to a curtained exam room. While I was waiting for the doctor, a little boy and his dad arrived in the space next to mine. I could clearly hear the boy's terror and pain in his high-decibel screams and cries. My heart went out to him. His father seemed unable to calm him.

When the nurse came in to check on me, I asked her about the child's injury. She told me the little guy had gotten a nasty gash from stepping on a sharp seashell and would need several stitches in his foot—when they could calm him down enough to make the repair.

I told her I was a first-grade teacher and mother of four and asked whether I could try to help. "I have a knack with kids, since I spend most of my time with them."

"Fine with me," the nurse said, "as long as his dad is okay with it. He looks like he could use some support."

I poked my head inside the curtain to the adjacent space, quickly introduced myself, and said, "I was next door, and I heard that a VERY BRAVE boy has a hurt foot!"

The young boy looked up at me, startled, his eyes brimming with tears. I moved toward him, stooping to his eye level. "Can you tell me what happened?"

Sniffling, and with great effort, the boy told me about his foray into the ocean, the awful pain, the blood.

"Oh my! Did you get bitten by a GREAT WHITE SHARK?" I asked, my eyes wide with mock fear.

He laughed, wiping at a tear. "No! It was a seashell! But a big, sharp one!"

"Can I look at it?" I asked.

He bravely showed me his wound. I had to admit, it wasn't pretty.

"Oh my goodness," I said. "That looks pretty painful. But look how brave you are! You are like a superhero, aren't you?"

The boy immediately smiled, sat up straight, and made a muscle with his thin little arm.

"Yes, I am like Superman! I'm strong!"

I squeezed his bicep, the size of a walnut, and gave him my most impressive, "Wow! You ARE strong!"

I glanced at the boy's dad. His face was filled with gratitude. "Are you an angel?" he asked.

I laughed and said, "No, just a mom and a teacher."

The father and the nurse asked whether I could stay and chat with the boy while they stitched him up. I readily agreed. All went well. The boy was fully focused on impressing me with his courage, and we chatted about all the Marvel superheroes and their powers—a subject on which he and I were both well versed.

As a wife, a mom of three boys, and now a grandmother of five grandsons, I know that the secret to connecting with males is pretty simple. All I did was call this frightened, crying little guy "a very brave boy." I spoke to his inner hero, reminding him of his most heroic qualities. It doesn't matter whether he is seven, twenty-seven, or sixty-seven; I have never met a male of any age who doesn't respond to the call to be a hero.

How well do you remember being a kid? Can you recall hanging by your knees from a jungle gym to show off your heroic skills for the benefit of others on the playground? There's a part of every man that will forever be a little boy trying to do something important and hoping others will notice and comment on what an amazing job he's done. As counselors, we can tell you, and you know it's true: Men never stop needing affirmation and admiration. It isn't vanity or a weakness; it's the way we're built.

The Bible is loaded with stories of heroes who are called out and revealed; who discover their true identity and are given missions of great significance to accomplish. Heroic sagas are universal. They hit us at the level of the human heart and inspire us on our journey through life. That's why men—at any age—never tire of hearing stories of heroes rising to the occasion.

One of the most affirming and humorous stories in the Old Testament is in Judges 6, where God tells the truth about a reluctant hero named Gideon and calls him to his true identity.

We meet Gideon as he is "threshing wheat at the bottom of a winepress to hide the grain from the Midianites."[4]

Typically, someone threshing wheat would do it out in the open so the wind could blow away the chaff. But Gideon is working in a winepress, likely a large stonework cylinder with walls and sides, hoping to avoid the attention of the Midianites, Israel's enemies of the hour, during one of many times when the nation turned its back on God and started worshiping false gods.

Let's summarize:

Gideon is a wheat farmer in a winepress.

He's hiding.

He's frightened.

So far none of this sounds very heroic, right?

But at that very moment, God sends "the angel of the

Lord" to appear to Gideon and say, "Mighty hero, the Lord is with you!"[5]

We love how God sees and focuses on our true identity. He has a special kind of x-ray vision that sees only the good and heroic in us. The messy stuff? The cowardly parts? The bent toward sin? It's all covered up by the grace and love of Christ. What God sees is the very best version of us, and he persistently calls it out of us until we, too, can see that we are brave warriors and sons of the King.

Press the pause button for a moment. Notice that the angel doesn't offer to swoop in and rescue Gideon and his people. Instead, he speaks to and validates the latent hero within Gideon's heart.

There's an important principle here: If you want to help a man find his way in life, don't immediately try to rescue him. Don't go into advice mode right away, telling him what to do. First appeal to his heroic soul, the mighty warrior inside the panicked, worried man. Validate and affirm his true identity and his innate abilities. Assure him that you trust his relationship with God and that—with God's help—he *will* find a solution to any problem life throws his way.

By the way, this is a vital tip for fathering teens and young adults. As you mentor them from boys to men, *validate* more, rescue less. Most men are quietly, inwardly *starving* for validation and encouragement from other men, especially elders and mentors and fathers. Affirmation is in short supply in the world where most men live and work.

Note as well that the angel breaks through Gideon's feelings of isolation and alienation. He assures him he is not alone or forsaken or forgotten. No matter how it might *feel*, God hasn't lost sight of him.

"The LORD is with you."[6]

In times of deep sorrow or discouragement, it is easy to forget that God is *with* us and *for* us. Always. Even when—no, *especially* when—life hurts.

As it turns out, Gideon has a few questions for the angel: "If the LORD is with us, why has all this happened to us? And where are all the miracles our ancestors told us about?"[7]

Gideon is in the presence of an angel, which you would think would be a bit daunting. But what do *we* know? We weren't there. And angels appear in many forms. We like to imagine this one dressed in the ancient-day equivalent of blue jeans because Gideon seems awfully at ease with him. Whatever the case, Gideon felt comfortable asking this angel some form of, "Hey, where is that 'wonderful plan for your life' we're supposed to have? Where is all the *winning?*"

What Gideon doesn't say, but is likely implying, is, "I'm hiding in this winepress, terrified of the bad guys because . . . well . . . uh . . . the God who sent you isn't doing his job! Where has he been, anyway? This is not the life we signed up for!"

Like a wise rabbi, the angel ignores the question and gives Gideon an order instead.

"Go . . . and save Israel."[8]

The angel could have reminded Gideon of how the Israelites had wandered away from God, and not the other way around; but he was there on a mission, not to engage in debate.

Therapists, too, sense when it is time to exit a nonproductive back-and-forth dialogue. When one of our callers on *New Life Live!* is stuck in his own head, arguing and playing point/counterpoint, we try to redirect him toward something positive and doable—anything to break the cycle of negative self-talk that stalls growth and limits change.

The brain can be like a dog with a bone, chewing the same old hard knuckle, digging it up again and again. To distract someone from habitual, undesirable thought loops, give him something positive and active to do. That will interrupt the endless cycle and allow fresh, healthier ways of thinking and feeling to occur naturally. It's kind of like throwing a brightly colored Frisbee near a dog who is chewing on a bone.

The angel interrupts Gideon's negative thought pattern with a new and adventurous action step: "Go in the strength you have and save Israel out of Midian's hand." Then he adds a question: "Am I not sending you?"[9]

Press the pause button again. The angel doesn't say, "If you really work at it, one day you'll have the strength you need to do mighty things." Rather, he tells Gideon to undertake this mission with the strength he *already has*. Men tend to forget the incredible power they have within themselves. If God lives in us, we have the Holy Spirit. We have within us—right here, right now—all we need to do everything we are called to do.

Sometimes we don't realize who we really are, or life wears us down and we get busy and distracted and simply forget. Like the little boy who stepped on the seashell and got lost in a flurry of pain and fear, bad circumstances can throw us into negative thought loops. A wise mentor will not try to rescue us. He will simply remind us of who we really are: true heroes, complete with all the divine power needed to accomplish what we are called to do, today and every day.[10]

When the angel asks, "Am I not sending you?" he implies, "I wouldn't be assigning you this mission if I didn't think you were ready and able, with the strength and courage of God within you."

You can read the rest of Gideon's story in Judges 6–8. It's full of action and insight, an entertaining and inspiring read. In the end, Gideon accomplishes what appears to be an impossible mission—routing an army of 135,000 swordsmen with only three hundred men, using trumpets and torches and the element of surprise.[11]

God's Spirit specifically guided, empowered, and instructed Gideon each step of the way, and Israel went on to enjoy forty years of peace, worshiping God instead of false idols, until Gideon's death.

Gideon's hero journey, his legendary saga, began when he was a frightened, discouraged, reluctant young man who decided to believe what the angel said about his true identity.

Greatness began to unfold, and the adventure of a lifetime commenced the moment Gideon embraced and believed the truth about who he was in God's eyes. He was already a mighty warrior with the strength and power of God within him. He just needed to be reminded and encouraged. He had to believe that God would partner with him, and then get on with the mission. No looking back.

What you do, what you have, what people say about you is not who you are. . . . You are a child of God, and the spiritual life starts when you proclaim that truth.

HENRI NOUWEN

Your True Identity: Beloved Son

One of the most moving experiences of my (Steve's) life was hearing Henri Nouwen, a well-known priest and author, speak in the early 1990s at The Foundation, a small gathering in Ontario, Canada. His message was on the return of the Prodigal Son, using Rembrandt's famous painting as a point of reference.[12] He explained how *both* sons in the story needed the father's grace—the prodigal younger brother, for obvious reasons; but also the elder brother, who was spiritually stunted by self-righteous pride.

It was a life-altering truth and insight for me, and Henri Nouwen became a spiritual hero in my life, though he didn't look much like a hero by most people's standards. Tall and gangly, with a long, kindly face framed by wavy silver hair, Nouwen spoke with a charming Dutch accent and gesticulated wildly to make his points with unbridled passion. This priest's vulnerable writings and lectures have been a guiding light to millions. He was a great hero of empathy and healing to countless souls.

Many of his bestselling books address the subject of Christian identity. Our belovedness and belonging were the central themes of Nouwen's passion and ministry. He called to who we truly are in the deep core of our being. His *Life of the Beloved* and *The Inner Voice of Love* are about discovering our identity and the spiritual practice of discerning the true voice of God, which is the voice of lavish, unconditional, abundant love.

Left to our own devices, Nouwen shared, we tend to define ourselves in one of three ways: by what we have, by what we do, or by what others think about us. Nouwen emphatically asserted that these definitions are false. In fact, they come from the voice of our enemy.

Jesus was tempted by Satan to do miraculous things (turn stones into bread, then leap off a cliff and let angels catch him) in order to gather riches and power and impress others—as if that would have any meaning to him, who, though going through a very rough patch in the desert, clearly understood his true identity: beloved Son of the Father in heaven.[13]

As the only begotten Son of Almighty God, Jesus already had everything he truly needed and wanted. He knew who he was, he was comfortable in his own skin, and he needed no showmanship or cheap tricks to prove it. Instead, he turned his back on all of Satan's temptations, recognizing them for what they were: lies from the ultimate con man, the same conniving snake who had whispered false promises to Adam and Eve in the Garden.

Here's a truth you can take to the bank: As an adopted son of Almighty God,[14] you already possess everything you truly need and want. "Your life is now hidden with Christ in God."[15] When you embrace your true identity, that of beloved child of the King, you don't need to impress anyone or prove your worth. The fact of your belovedness and belonging should center, calm, strengthen, and encourage you.

Immediately before the wilderness temptation, Jesus had been baptized in the Jordan River by his cousin John. On this special occasion, God revealed his Son's true identity to all who were gathered. In God's own words, spoken from heaven, he said of Jesus, "This is my Son, whom I love; with him I am well pleased."[16] God told Jesus that his favor rested on him. Jesus was already a hero to his Father, and he didn't have to do a thing to earn it.

These are affirmations that boys long to hear from their fathers and important male mentors:

- "I love you."
- "You belong to my heart forever."
- "I believe in you."
- "I admire you, just as you are—which, by the way, is awesome."

Hearing affirmations like these, early and often, helps a boy form his core identity as a beloved son. When life gets hard and he gets hurt, or when temptations arise, his ego may get battered and bruised. But as he returns to the central truths of his belonging and his belovedness, his true identity will grow stronger and stronger within his heart. He has a spiritual core, a calm internal place to which he can return again and again when storms of discouragement blow his way. Sure, hurtful things may sting a spiritually centered man, but assaults from others won't debilitate him or take him out of the game. As the apostle Paul observed, "We get knocked down, but we are not destroyed."[17]

My friend, when you know your identity in Christ, you become very clear about fact versus falsehood. You know you are not who people say you are. You are not what you have or what you own. You are not what you do. You are not the sum of your mistakes. You are a son of the King, loved beyond measure. Nothing you do can make the Father love you more; nothing you do will make him love you less. If you have a child of your own, you've had a small glimpse of this kind of love from the Father's perspective.

False Identities

In his book *Life of the Beloved*, Henri Nouwen writes,

> Self-rejection is the greatest enemy of the spiritual life because it contradicts the sacred voice that calls

us the "Beloved." Being the Beloved expresses the
core truth of our existence. . . .

Though the experience of being the Beloved
has never been completely absent from my life,
I never claimed it as my core truth. I kept running
around it in large or small circles, always looking
for someone or something able to convince me of
my Belovedness. . . .

Aren't you, like me, hoping that some person,
thing or event will come along to give you that final
feeling of inner well-being you desire? Don't you
often hope: "May this book, idea, course, trip, job,
country or relationship fulfill my deepest desire." . . .

The world tells you many lies about who you are,
and you simply have to be realistic enough to remind
yourself of this. Every time you feel hurt, offended or
rejected, you have to dare to say to yourself: "These
feelings, strong as they may be, are not telling me
the truth about myself. The truth, even though I
cannot feel it right now, is that I am the chosen child
of God, precious in God's eyes, called the Beloved
from all eternity and held safe in an everlasting
embrace."[18]

Meditate on that last sentence until the truth of it begins
to seep into your inner being.

Breathe it in.

Bask in it.

Resonate with it.

Whether you feel it right now or not, the truth is that *you are a chosen child of God, precious in his eyes, called beloved from all eternity, and held safe in an everlasting embrace.*

As the apostle Paul writes in Galatians 2:20, "My old self has been crucified with Christ. It is no longer I who live, but Christ lives in me. So I live in this earthly body by trusting in the Son of God, who loved me and gave himself for me."

Take on the identity of Christ, the Beloved Son in whom the Father—*your* Father—is well pleased. When the enemy whispers lies about your identity, go back to the truth again and again—that your identity is God's beloved boy.

Just as Frank Reagan said to his family, God also says to you: "This family does not stand down. Ever." God will never stop being the Father who stands by you, stands with you, and calls you by name.

The late author and speaker Brennan Manning echoed many of Henri Nouwen's themes in his writings and ministry. Though Manning struggled with the pull of alcoholism most of his life, he held tightly to his central identity as a beloved son of the Father, even when from time to time he got lost in the mire of his disease. He once said, "*God loves you unconditionally, as you are and not as you should be, because nobody is as they should be.*"[19]

Your unshakable identity as a beloved son of God is the supernatural anchor for anything you do of significance, for anything that leaves a legacy of meaning—not because you are perfect, but because you belong to the heart of God. You are his child, come what may.

My deepest awareness of myself is that I am deeply loved by Jesus Christ and I have done nothing to earn it or deserve it.

BRENNAN MANNING, *THE RAGAMUFFIN GOSPEL*

Living in God's Love

Jesus used the phrase "abide in me" to describe the relationship he wants with us.[20] The word *abide* carries the sense of settling in and making yourself at home. Rest easy. Put your feet up. You are God's beloved child. Welcome to the family dinner table, to the place where your soul always knows and feels its worth, no matter what happens in the world around you.

If you're prone to forget, as we often are, repeat this truth to yourself until it becomes an abiding part of your consciousness: "I am loved by my heavenly Father. I am loved by my heavenly Father. I am loved by my heavenly Father." Sometimes it takes a lot of repetition to counter the negative voices in our memories.

Beloved of the Father is the truth of who you are. It is the real man behind the mask.

God loves you. God is love. We hear this a lot. But what does it look like? What does it feel like?

One of my (Steve's) friends was out riding a horse one

day when it bucked him off into a metal gate, caving in his skull, instantly blinding his left eye, and breaking a slew of bones in his body. He spent the next two years in the hospital, enduring more than twenty operations, before he could go home again.

Those who were with my friend at the time of the accident said that as he hit the ground, he began to scream and shout, twisting and turning violently from the pain. Then, in the next instant, he quietly settled down, not moving, and a look of peace came over his face. Everyone thought he was dying or was maybe already dead. They knew not to touch him or move him, but it took almost an hour for the Life Flight helicopter to arrive.

My friend later told me that, in those moments, he felt the presence of God as he had never felt it before or since. It was like a color, a beautiful purple glow, and all he felt in the presence of God was love—pure, strong, eternal, immeasurable love. This love so enveloped him that it overpowered anything wrong he had ever done in his past, calmed every fear he had in the present, and overcame his intense pain.

He felt the Lord speak to him, telling him not to worry and that he would not die but recover. He also felt God impress a verse of Scripture on his heart: "The LORD giveth and the LORD taketh away. Blessed be the name of the LORD."[21] My friend believes this was in reference to his blind eye, which was not repairable.

My friend experienced the supernatural love of God, and

its power was so much stronger than the sins of his past, which were irrelevant in the brilliance of God's divine and powerful love.

Do you believe God loves you this much? If not, I hope you will start to trust the amazing staying power of his grace and love.

"And I am convinced that nothing can ever separate us from God's love. Neither death nor life, neither angels nor demons, neither our fears for today nor our worries about tomorrow—not even the powers of hell can separate us from God's love."[22]

What's in a Name?

One day Jesus asked his disciples, "Who do people say that I am?" The disciples tossed out a variety of options they had heard from the people around them. Some thought Jesus was John the Baptist, back from the dead. Others said he was Elijah. Some said he was one of the other prophets.

Then Jesus looked at Peter and asked, "Who do you say I am?"

Peter replied, "You are the Messiah, the Son of the living God."

Bingo! *Ding ding ding!* Give that man a prize!

Jesus gave Peter an A+ for his answer and called him blessed, because God the Father had revealed to him Christ's true identity.

Jesus then used this discussion as a stepping-stone to help

Peter claim a new identity from God. Peter's given name was Simon, which derives from the Hebrew word *shema* ("to hear"). But from then on, Jesus told his beloved disciple he would be known as Peter, or Petros in the Greek, which means "rock." What man wouldn't stand a little taller being called The Rock? (Look at the movie star who adopted that name—his self-esteem looks pretty intact.)

Jesus went on to describe the meaning and the mission that would accompany Peter's new name. He would become an influential leader among the "called-out ones" (*ekklesia*) and would use his spiritual authority and power for good.[23]

But Peter would need every drop of power available to him because his life wasn't going to get easier. He would falter at times—at really important times—and he would sometimes seem to be anything but a rock. Three times he denied that he even knew Jesus, shortly before the Crucifixion.[24] But Jesus forgave Peter and reminded him of his true identity and mission. He is patient and persistent like that. In fact, when Jesus appeared beside the Sea of Galilee in his resurrected body, he gave Peter a chance to verbally affirm his love for him three times—once for each of the denials. And Jesus asked Peter—again three times—to do something for him, to take on a mission of great importance: "Feed my sheep."[25]

As he was about to depart for heaven, Jesus, the Good Shepherd, commissioned Peter to feed the sheep that Jesus loved so deeply. In other words, Jesus wanted Peter to nourish his followers by teaching them to love, forgive, and encourage one another.

It's also interesting to observe that Jesus never said anything directly to Peter about messing up so completely and publicly. There was no berating, no "I'm so disappointed in you" admonitions. Jesus simply reminded Peter of their mutual love and gave him a fresh addendum to his mission. In so doing, Jesus said to Peter, "You know I love you, and I know you love me. All is forgiven. Relationship restored. Now we have work to do, a vital mission to accomplish."

I (Steve) can't help but think back to the scene of Aslan speaking privately to Edmund and then refusing to let anyone mention Edmund's failures again. Edmund was back on track. He was a prince. Time to get on with being princely!

But as those of us who have experienced divine grace know, we are changed by such lavish mercy and love. Thereafter everything we do has more humility and gratitude attached to it. In truth, our pride dissolves, and we become much more tolerable, approachable, and authentic.

Here's a revealing and encouraging prayer exercise: Ask God to give you a new name, one to go along with your first name—*Beloved*.

We know a man named Brian who lost years of his life to a drug addiction. He prayed about his identity and sensed God telling him, "You have been calling yourself 'Broken' for years. But I call you 'Healer.' You are a beloved Healer."

Brian began to write a new "identity narrative," or inner story, for his life. He saw that none of his past pain in life, none of his struggles, would be wasted if given to God to be used for good. God used all of Brian's past failures and heartaches to widen his compassion and deepen his understanding of others who are in pain.

Brian began to find unique ways to heal and grow and recover. As he got help, he became "strong at the broken places" and encouraged other hurting folks in their healing journeys.[26] In time, Brian became an addiction counselor. Addicts trusted him because they knew he understood their unique struggles, and they found hope because Brian was living in his new identity, attaching himself to a new name, and embracing a new story to go with it.

It isn't what happens to us in life that determines how we experience our unfolding story. It is how we *think* about what happens to us. Our perspective changes everything, and a fresh perspective can turn a vital switch in our brains and alter the trajectory of the rest of our lives. Nothing can give a man a fresh perspective and a new lease on life like claiming a new identity. One way to do it is to take any negative name you call yourself (or that someone in your past has called you), any name that is holding you back, and exchange it for a name that bubbles up from the truth of who you are, the way God sees you.

We believe this concept can be life altering for you. Take some time in the next few days—today, if possible—to walk and talk with God. You already know your first name is Beloved—your identity is settled and you are God's child, completely loved. But ask him for a second name, like a nick-name just between you and him, and see what happens.

Your new name might come to you as you walk or later as you read Scripture. It could come in a song or as a word from someone else out of the blue. Be open and receptive. God is very creative in how he speaks to his kids.

The true name is one which expresses the character, the nature, the being, the meaning of the person who bears it. It is the man's own symbol—his soul's picture. . . . Who can give a man this, his own name? God alone.

GEORGE MacDONALD, "THE NEW NAME," *UNSPOKEN SERMONS*

When God gives you your new name, let that new iden-tity soak into your spirit and your life. As it does, you will be transformed. Over time it will change how you relate to others as well.

It might help to write down the name or names that the belittling voices of doom, gloom, and ridicule have called you in the past. These will serve as a point of contrast. Perhaps you recall the name that bullies called you at school or an abusive parent used when he or she was angry. Maybe there is a false and demeaning name you automatically call yourself when you mess up. Ask God for a contrasting, true name—a better name, a great and uplifting name to take its place.

Scripture and hymns often use metaphors from the natural world to describe God: Lion of Judah, Fount of Every Blessing, Light of the World. Word pictures easily sink deep into our memory, and such vivid images are powerful in helping us overcome limiting labels from our past.

So before you move on to the next chapter, take time to pray and ponder your true identity in Christ—the person you really are at the core—covered by grace, empowered by the Holy Spirit. Allow the Spirit to give you a word picture and a unique nickname to describe how God sees your soul, the valiant warrior that may have been hiding until now. Ask for a name that will encourage you, expand your vision, and prepare you for the next stage of your hero's journey.

3

THE DAD FACTOR

Heroic Secret #3: Men Need Mentors

Dads are most ordinary men turned by love into heroes,
adventurers, story-tellers, singers of songs.

PAM BROWN

Two of the most powerful words I hear when I listen to men's stories both start with the letter *W*. One of those words is a stand-alone question: *Why?*

Three chapters into a book on male heroism, maybe you're quietly asking yourself, *Why am I not feeling like a hero? Why do I feel as if other guys grasp what true manhood is, but I'm not getting it? Why am I not finding the great life that a man is supposed to live? Why do I feel like I'm half man, half question mark?*

The answer to those questions is very likely a second powerful word that starts with *W: wounded*. Most often, that wounding comes from a father who loved his son but was (or is) inept at expressing his love in a meaningful way.

In a perfect world, we would all have fathers and be perfect fathers. But we don't have to tell you this isn't a perfect world. We're still a long way from heaven on earth.

Every boy, in his journey to become a man, takes an arrow in the center of his heart, in the place of his strength. Because the wound is rarely discussed and even more rarely healed, every man carries a wound. And the wound is nearly always given by his father.

JOHN ELDREDGE, *WILD AT HEART*

First Aid for Father Wounds

Our heavenly Father is the ultimate mentor. In the previous chapter, we asked you to contemplate his eternal love for you and your true identity of belonging and acceptance—how he is delighted with you and proud of you. We asked you to rename yourself as God's beloved and to ask God for a personal nickname—one that's just between you and him and invigorates the heroic soul within you.

Our earthly fathers, if they are good ones, make it easy to imagine the love of our heavenly Father. But perhaps you, like so many guys, did not have a great dad. Maybe your father was not at all what you'd call a hero figure in your life.

My father died when I (Dave) was twenty-three. As I mentioned earlier, he was not a great dad—often absent (in spirit, if not physically) and sometimes abusive. I didn't really grieve my father as a young man, and for a long time I didn't realize I had a father wound that needed some tending and mending. For the most part, I just avoided thoughts and memories of my dad. However, when I found myself behaving with my own sons in some of the same hurtful ways my father had behaved with me—as if I were on emotional autopilot—I knew it was time to take a good look at the past so I could be set free to be a more present and loving dad. I knew that I did not want to unconsciously pass these hurtful flaws and traits on to my kids.

My profession has allowed me to stay in regular contact with wonderful therapists over the years, and I received great help from my mentors. As a result, I have a huge heart for men who want to make peace with their dad—or the memory of their dad. I've written two books on the subject, and I've given a great deal of time, thought, and real-life practice toward helping men get free and move forward after a painful past with their parents. If this is a struggle for you, I highly recommend that you invest whatever time it takes and get whatever professional or spiritual help you need to make peace with your childhood and your dad. I'd like to share a few ways to begin healing from a painful childhood that may help nudge you along.

The place to start healing a father wound is by facing what was said and done to you. Take whatever negative memory pops into your mind and speak the truth about it. It is especially helpful to do this aloud in the presence of a counselor, therapist, or pastor—or someone else who is gifted in focused listening and will listen with compassion and understanding.

For this step, you may also want a companion there to simply acknowledge the reality of the hurt that happened to you as a boy or teen. Therapists sometimes call this person a *compassionate witness*. You will be amazed at how healing it is to have someone who can simply—but deeply and attentively—listen to your stories, understand your "war wounds," acknowledge the wrongs done to you and the pain you've experienced, and provide some comfort if these memories bring up angry or sorrowful emotions.

This is important: If you were very seriously abused by your father or think you may have PTSD, please do this exercise in the presence of a professional therapist who specializes in trauma and healing. You will need someone who can help you pace the process—a little at a time—so it doesn't become overwhelming.

Some men are able to process old pain by writing down the memories—purging them, if you will, from their minds. By getting the old painful scene and accompanying emotions down on paper, some men experience more relief than they do from only talking about a traumatic memory.

The next step is to share or write what *should* have been said, what *should* have happened if your father had been emotionally healthy. Then imagine yourself now—as an adult—saying to the child you once were what should have been said and done.

Another approach is to visualize Jesus saying these truthful and comforting words to you. Often a good counselor, therapist, or relationally wise mentor can provide this feedback for you. He can say to you the things your father should have said in a variety of circumstances. What you are doing, in essence, is providing a memory *overlay*—taking a strong and positive visual or verbal picture of truth and superimposing it over a memory of a time when you were told cruel and false stories about yourself. In this way, the painful memory loosens its grip as God's truth takes over.

When men are given appropriate compassion and receive acknowledgment that what happened to them was wrong and unjust, the painful sting in the memories often begins to ease. If you will pause long enough to give yourself the self-care you need to heal, the memories may begin to lose their hold on you, usually without a lot of effort on your part.

The more you practice caring for yourself and speaking truth, the more the old voices of negativity will fade and lose their power. You'll still remember the past, but the anger or hurt may fade. When you are in a better emotional place and have compassionately tended to your heart, it could be time to move on to the next step: forgiveness. But don't rush this step. If you're unsure whether you're ready, wait until you feel lighter and stronger and more certain of your worth and identity in Christ.

How Do We Forgive?

Where do we start? It helps to understand that forgiveness doesn't mean that the harm done to you or the terrible things said to you are okay. They're not. But when you forgive, you no longer hold on to those memories like a dog with a bone, because they no longer affect you in the present. In other words, you don't need those memories and the accompanying anxiety and anger anymore. Up until now, you've been kidnapped and held back by them. But no more. Now you know that you are God's beloved. You are centered in your true identity. From this place of strength, security, and freedom, you can let go of the need to punish or hurt your father with revenge or angry thoughts.

It may be helpful to look at your father's past to see what challenges, hurts, mental illness, addictions, or trauma he faced that led him to his flawed way of fathering. Another way to move toward forgiving your father is to try to imagine him as a child and then forgive the hurting child he once was, the boy who grew up to hurt others. As the saying goes,

"Hurting people hurt people." This is often true of flawed, absent, or abusive fathers.

I (Dave) find it is usually easier for men to begin to forgive their parents as the imagined children they once were. Then they can slowly forgive them at other ages and stages, moving up to the present moment. Allow this process to take whatever time it takes. The deeper and longer and more pervasive the abuse, the longer it usually takes for forgiveness to happen. You can't rush the process.

In my practice over the years, I often counseled men who grew up with a father who had survived the horrors of World War II or Vietnam. Many returning soldiers had untreated PTSD and turned to alcohol or drugs to medicate their pain. These dads often became stoic, silent, and distant or had sudden bouts of anger and rage. Many soldiers feel they left part of themselves on the battlefield. Some suffered head injuries that affected their ability to control their temper or think clearly. Understanding what these fathers suffered has been helpful to their sons and daughters, who grew up in their unpredictable or silent shadows. It doesn't erase the harm done or the painful memories, but it does help the process of forgiveness.

Then there is the really big picture: We are all flawed. None of us is perfect. We all have things we regret. We all need a Hero Savior. It is easier to forgive others when we understand the great gift of grace we ourselves have been given.

If your father is still living, should you have a healing conversation with him? Perhaps. If you decide to do it, I highly recommend you prepare for it with a counselor, pastor, or wise friend. Have a plan in mind for what you will do if it does not go as well as you hope. Maybe you can start by writing a letter, one that you let sit for a while, and then have a trusted mentor read through it before you send it.

If your dad is no longer living, maybe you can still write a letter to him, releasing him and forgiving him. You may want to keep the letter in a safe place, burn it on a campfire in a special spot, or dispose of it through some other ritual that is meaningful to you. I also recommend that you read some of the books Steve and I have written on the subject of healing father-son relationships:

> *Making Peace with Your Father* (Revell, 2004)
> *Healing Is a Choice* (Thomas Nelson, 2011)
> *Forgiving What You'll Never Forget* (Revell, 2017)
> *Take Your Life Back: How to Stop Letting the Past and Other People Control You* (Tyndale Momentum, 2016)

Father to the fatherless, defender of widows—this is God, whose dwelling is holy. God places the lonely in families.

PSALM 68:5-6

The Miracle of Mentors

If you had an absent or abusive dad—a dad who was dealing with an unbalanced brain, addictions, or unhealed wounds from his past—you may have had to look for other mentors or father figures to fill in the gaps that your earthly father left wide open. But even if you had the world's best dad, he was still a finite, imperfect, flawed, and limited man.

It never hurts to have at least one, if not several, fatherly men on your team as you go through life. All men fare better with mentors on their journey. Most mentors or father figures will play an important role in your life at a critical juncture, helping you through a certain challenge or period of time. A youth director. A high school coach. A college professor. An uncle or a grandfather. A great boss. A pastor or counselor. Some rare men might take on a fatherly role toward you for as long as they live. Such was the case with Fred Rogers—yes, the famous Mister Rogers—and a journalist named Tim Madigan.[1]

In his honest and touching memoir, *I'm Proud of You*, Madigan, longtime reporter for the *Fort Worth Star-Telegram*, shares poignantly of his unlikely friendship with Fred Rogers, the beloved children's television host and Presbyterian minister. Fred was not the image of a superhero most men would conjure up. But this unassuming, loving, soft-spoken, and wise man, who wore sneakers and a cardigan, turned out to have a profound impact on not only millions of children but also many adults in search of a father's blessing.

At one of the lowest points in his life, Tim Madigan interviewed Mr. Rogers. Tim had grown up with a judgmental father he felt could never please, and this wound seemed to haunt him. He was depressed, self-absorbed, and heading for divorce.

In the presence of Fred Rogers, however, Tim felt wholly loved, embraced, delighted in, accepted, and affirmed by a father figure for the first time in his life. Rogers was more than a kids' television friend; he was a man of deep spiritual grounding who purposely prioritized loving the people from all ages, races, backgrounds, abilities, and walks of life that he came in contact with. You could say that expressing God's love was Mr. Rogers's superpower. Sharing that love through healing conversations was his mission.

From a young age, Tim Madigan was a person of words and sensitivity, while his dad was a man of long silences and physicality. When his dad did speak, it was often in harsh and belittling ways. The lack of his dad's affirmation and approval affected every aspect of Tim's life. In a letter to Fred Rogers in 1996, he wrote, "The anger toward my father—anger from the past—threatens to consume me at times, and makes healthy loving and living very difficult." Then he added, "My prayer is now, Fred, that the Lord will soften my heart."[2]

At another time of depression and vulnerability, Tim wrote to ask Fred to be his spiritual mentor and the person in his life who would be proud of him.

Fred Rogers wrote back:

Dear Tim,
The answer to your question is
  "YES."
  A resounding YES . . .

*I will be proud of you. I am proud of you. I have
been proud of you since first we met. I'm deeply touched
. . . and look forward to knowing all that you would
care to share in the future. Nothing you could tell
me would change my YES for you. Please remember
that.*[3]

This life-altering letter of unconditional love and affirmation initiated seven years of correspondence and friendship between the two men. In each letter to Tim, Fred
included the acronym IPOY, which stood for I'm Proud
of You.

Their communication was honest, real, and surprisingly
spiritual. "I'm fairly convinced that the Kingdom of God is
for the broken-hearted," Fred Rogers wrote. "You write of
'powerlessness.' Join the club, we are not in control: God is."[4]

Rogers always found a way to be inclusive of others and
never put himself above anyone. This aspect of his personality was extremely healing for Tim Madigan.

During those years, with mentoring from Fred and other
good men, Tim made peace with his father and healed many
of the old wounds. His marriage, too, was restored.

In his book *The World according to Mister Rogers*, Fred
Rogers wrote about what might be called hero moments on
earth and what they can look like in real life.

In the external scheme of things, shining moments
are as brief as the twinkling of an eye, yet such

twinklings are what eternity is made of—moments when we human beings can say "I love you," "I'm proud of you," "I forgive you," "I'm grateful for you." That's what eternity is made of: invisible, imperishable *good stuff.*[5]

Indeed, the stuff of heroes sometimes looks more like a welcoming, honest, accepting, spiritual friendship than zapping a bad guy into the atmosphere.

Tim Madigan's book surprised, touched, and inspired men from all walks of life because father-son wounds and father-son healing stories are so central in the development of a man's character. The long-lasting emotional impact and ongoing popularity of *Field of Dreams*, the classic father-son baseball movie, is just one example of this deep male longing to reunite with their dads, to play just one more game of catch at twilight. Burly men weep at that father-and-son-playing-catch scene in the movie. It touches a powerful chord.

When our fathers don't fulfill this kind of role in our lives, we need other role models who will reflect to us the love of both our heavenly Father and an earthly father. It's great when these can be in-the-flesh fatherly men; but if you're a reader, good books about great men with hearts after God can also heal and mentor us.

We want to emphasize that the absence of a good father is so deep and so profound in a boy's or a man's life that it usually takes more than one or two fatherly men and mentors over the course of a lifetime to fill in the giant gap left by one absent or abusive father.

Even if you had a great dad, having other men on your team as you go through life will elevate your experiences like nothing else can. Here's the deal though. You may have to be vulnerable and ask someone you admire whether they will meet with you once a month (or more often) to offer good advice and empathy. That's not necessarily an easy thing to do when you have felt the sting of rejection at such a deep level. But you must be brave and seek and ask until you find men who will mentor you in areas where you feel you missed something of value, something a man can only get from another good, wise male.

Jim Daly is president and CEO of Focus on the Family, an international Christian organization dedicated to helping families thrive. And he is one of my (Dave's) best buddies. For a lot of reasons, there are not many men in ministry whom I truly enjoy hanging out with. Some are focused on pretense and keeping up an image or facade. At the other end of the spectrum are leaders who are crass, characterless, bitter, or even vindictive. Jim Daly doesn't belong in either of those categories. I love being with him because he is a great leader and a great man, and he has a very fun spirit along with his heart for God. At almost any convention we attend together, we somehow manage to pull away from the crowd and find a quiet corner in a restaurant where we can share openly and honestly with each other. We laugh, maybe cry, and enjoy just being who we are. I always walk away a better man and so full of respect for Jim. Knowing his story makes me respect him all the more.

For much of his childhood, Jim was an orphan and a foster child. Abandoned by his alcoholic father at the tender age of five, Jim lost his mom to cancer just four years later. His stepfather, completely overcome with grief, abandoned the family right after the funeral, leaving Jim and his four older siblings to fend for themselves. Many tough years followed, including time in foster care, before Jim found good, caring male mentors and role models. These men helped him find meaning, belonging, and purpose in life.

In his memoir, *Finding Home*, Jim writes, "I am convinced that no matter how torn up the road has already been, or how pothole-infested the road may look ahead, nothing—*nothing*— is impossible for God. . . . I'm living proof."[6]

Show me a successful individual and I'll show you someone who had real positive influences in his or her life. I don't care what you do for a living—if you do it well I'm sure there was someone cheering you on or showing the way. A mentor.

DENZEL WASHINGTON

Jim's football coach, Paul Moro, was perhaps his most significant influence, taking him under his wing and investing in his life on and off the field. It was Paul who helped Jim come to faith in Christ. Jim is convinced that the gift of a good mentor is priceless, and he is eternally grateful for the male mentors who filled in so many of the father gaps in his life. Because of Jim's background and his ability to understand on a gut level what it feels like to be without a father and a family, he brings a remarkable credibility, kindness, and authenticity to his work at Focus on the Family, as well as to his family, his friends, and others he encounters in his everyday life.

Me? A Mentor?

If you have been blessed with a good father or some great mentors in your life, consider paying it forward. Become a mentor to someone who needs what you have to offer. Don't worry about being perfect—that is *not* a requirement. When you help and encourage another man on his journey, you will receive just as much or more in return. God designed our brains to release feel-good neurotransmitters when we help others; we are hardwired to be everyday heroes.

Our friend Dustin and his wife, Shawna, once led a young-marrieds group at their local church. They would often get calls from newlywed husbands who suddenly realized they were out of their wheelhouse in knowing how to be a good husband to a very real wife. As Dustin tells it,

> One night we got a call from a husband who had, earlier that evening, suggested that his wife might not want to eat the second cookie she had picked up off the plate. As he explained it, "She said she was

trying to get in shape." He thought his young wife would appreciate his help with self-discipline. To his shock, she had locked herself in the bedroom instead and wouldn't talk to him or come out.

"What do I do?" he asked desperately. "What did I say that was so bad? Help!"

Most couples don't know what they don't know until they are in the throes of a real-life marriage. Premarital counseling can take you only so far. A newlywed man needs a mentor during his first and second year of marriage—when he is learning how to love and relate to his wife every single day—more than at any other time before.

Dustin went on to say,

After helping to calm that first crisis in literally the first week of their young marriage, I began meeting with this young husband for breakfast once a week, listening to the challenges he was facing and giving him what we laughingly called Husband Lessons. He shared that when he was a kid, his dad had divorced and never remarried, so he had no clue how to be a good husband. I passed along the tips and helps that I'd learned from my failures and successes and from my own good mentors in life. I encouraged him and sent him back home to his wife with fresh perspective and new practical ways to listen to and love her.

Dustin helped this young newlywed, and then to his surprise, God sent one young husband after another to him for help.

For five years, my mission turned out to be
mentoring young men, newly married, who
had no husbanding skills. Most had never seen
a healthy marriage in their home as a kid and
were just flailing around trying to figure it out
on their own. It was deeply satisfying. A decade
later, I still stay in touch with most of these men,
and their marriages are thriving. Even if they hit
a bump after all these years, they know they can
call me for honest feedback, prayer, and help. I
was able to help and encourage these great guys at
a crucial time in their lives, and I feel so blessed
and honored to have made a difference. Many of
them had abusive, absent, or silent fathers, and I
know that as I encouraged them in their marriages,
I became a father figure for a season of their
journeys.

You might expect that Dustin's parents were the perfect happy couple. You'd be dead wrong. When Dustin was thirteen, his father divorced his mom, leaving her for another woman. It devastated his happy childhood and broke his mom's heart. His parents each went on to have several other relationships and unhealthy marriages. His mother, thankfully, met a good man who was a great husband to her in the last decade of her life.

"When I came to Christ at age nineteen," Dustin said, "I vowed to do marriage differently. I got mentors. I read every book I could on how to be a good Christian husband."

But even with all the good mentoring and input Dustin received, his first marriage ended in divorce. The reasons are long and complicated and painful. It lasted nearly three decades before the wheels came off, but there was no real intimacy in the preceding decades.

"I was so lonely. I tried so hard to connect; I tried all I knew. She didn't believe in or want to go to counseling. I sank into depression and despair. I know I wasn't perfect. Far from it. But there is nothing like feeling alone in a marriage. The pain is hard to describe unless you've personally experienced it. I never thought I'd bomb at the one thing I most wanted to do and do well," Dustin said. "I felt like such a failure."

But God wasn't finished with Dustin. He married again. He took into account lessons from his failed marriage and lessons he'd gleaned from mentors and books, and it yielded a healthy and very happy second marriage to Shawna. They are about to celebrate the happiest twenty years of their lives with a trip to France.

"My marriage is great. Fabulous, even," Dustin shared with us. "But Shawna has PTSD, so I've had to learn a new set of husbanding skills to support her healing. Life and relationships are all about learning and growing, aren't they?

It never stops. But my wife is deeply committed to me, and I am committed to her. And Shawna desires intimacy in marriage, in all the senses of that word, as much as I do. It has made all the difference. We laugh a lot, are naturally affectionate, and have so much fun. And we work through all the challenges that come at us year by year. Challenges and figuring out healthy ways to deal with them will always be a part of human married life. We never arrive at perfection!"

Dustin continued. "The fact that God used me—a man from a divorced home, a man who had a divorce in his background—to mentor newly married guys . . . it seemed like a crazy miracle. But you know what these young men would say to me? They'd tell me that because I wasn't from a perfect home, and because I had experienced heartache and failure in marriage, they felt at ease telling me the truth about their lives. They felt hope that they, too, could make their marriages work."

The thing about being a mentor is that God often uses the most unlikely people to lead and mentor others. Remember Gideon? Remember Peter? You don't have to be perfect. You don't need to have an impressive background or spiritual pedigree. You just have to show up, roll up your sleeves, and offer to be a "wounded healer"—someone who knows pain, has experienced grace, and has made a little progress.

Dustin's unlikely "hero's mission" unfolded for him naturally. He was willing to help others in any way God wanted to use him. Before and after church, he'd pray for God to give him what he called divine appointments, encounters from the Holy Spirit where he might be a vessel to encourage someone. Dustin didn't go out seeking to help newlywed men learn husbanding skills; he would not have thought himself qualified. But God knew otherwise.

We have found that when you are open to being a mentor, God will naturally help unfold your mission without a lot of effort and fanfare. (More on finding your mission in the next chapter.) All you have to do is keep your eyes open, have a heart that is willing to be a vessel for God's love and encouragement, and keep your schedule open enough for breakfast or lunch meetings on a regular basis—weekly, biweekly, or monthly. Perfection is not required. Showing up with honesty and encouragement and sharing what has worked for you is all that's needed. Simply be a real friend and listen—because most of all, people long to be seen, heard, and deeply listened to. The art of paying rapt attention to another human being and asking good questions is unbelievably rare. Those who learn this skill will always be in demand, as there is no end to the number of men who need a safe place to unburden their hearts and receive honesty, compassion, and encouragement.

In Love's service, only the wounded can serve.

THORNTON WILDER, *THE ANGEL THAT TROUBLED THE WATERS*

Such a friend, such a mentor, does not require a degree or professional training. God may call you to get good training, but he requires only that you open your heart, your life, and some bits of time to encourage someone with what you have learned from your wisdom, your wins, and your wounds.

• • •

Fathering takes on many looks, many faces. Sometimes it looks like a biological dad passing on encouragement and guy stuff—manly know-how—to his son. But fathering can also look like a coach taking time to encourage a discouraged team member. Or like a youth minister taking a downcast teen out for coffee or on a hike. Or like a kind, patient boss mentoring an employee through a tough problem at work. Or like you, noticing that your kid's friend doesn't have a dad around, including him on fishing trips, teaching him how to throw a football, and telling him what a great kid he is.

If you have leftover father wounds and find yourself either avoiding them or thinking a lot about them, or if you start seeing some of your father's hurtful ways coming out in your own behavior, take a time-out and tend to those wounds. Doing so is one of the best decisions you can make because it will free you up to be the best dad or mentor you can be. There is an old saying that when one person heals, it results in healing for seven generations that follow. Your kids, grandkids, and great-grandkids are worth it. The more whole and healed you are, the more likely they will be too. Think of yourself as someone who stops to repair a broken bridge so that the loved ones who follow after you won't trip and fall at the same broken place.

If your father wound is affecting your quality of life, your self-esteem, or your relationships, it is never too late to deal with it. We have counseled men in their sixties and seventies who eventually found freedom from the burden of painful memories they carried for decades. As they healed, their relationships improved, and they had much more peace and confidence about leaving a good legacy for their loved ones.

In the hero's journey, almost every man will come to a crossroads called Father Wounds. One option is to ignore the wound when the old pain crops up. You can continue limping along, possibly wounding others as you lurch about on unsteady feet. The other, far better option is to take the road toward healing the father wound—pausing for deep and lasting repairs before moving onward and upward with renewed strength and joy for the journey ahead, steady on your feet. When you make peace with your earthly father, or with your memories of your earthly father, you will come to feel more deeply and eternally loved by your heavenly Father. That's true freedom.

What marvelous love the Father has extended to us! Just look at it—we're called children of God! That's who we *really* are.[7]

1 JOHN 3:1, MSG

4

SIDEKICKS FOR THE SOUL JOURNEY

Heroic Secret #4: You're Gonna Need Brothers

You can trust us to stick to you through thick and thin—to the bitter end. And you can trust us to keep any secret of yours—closer than you keep it yourself. But you cannot trust us to let you face trouble alone, and go off without a word. We are your friends.

J. R. R. TOLKIEN, *THE FELLOWSHIP OF THE RING*

I f you've watched the HBO series *Band of Brothers*, you might recall one of the Easy Company soldiers named Don Malarkey. In his autobiography, *Easy Company Soldier*, Malarkey writes of being in the bitter cold at the Battle of the Bulge and watching two friends writhe in the bloodied snow, each having lost a leg in a shelling. Afterward, huddled around a campfire with a handful of others, he receives the news that his best friend has been killed in combat. Distraught and freezing, he considers pulling the trigger of his holstered pistol and putting a bullet through his foot. With such a wound, he'd be of no use to the unit and would likely be sent back to England. His "accident" would remove him from this icy hell.

But he doesn't shoot himself. Why not? Because he realizes he is *necessary* to the other men. "If I'd put that bullet through my leg or gone to pieces . . . what would it have done to the rest of these guys?"[1]

We may not have seen combat or experienced the physical testing that Don Malarkey and others endured during World War II, but at some point in our lives, haven't we felt as if we were at a breaking point? Haven't we all reached a point where we were "hanging on to whatever shred of resolve we still had in us"?[2]

Don Malarkey didn't take the so-called easy way out; instead he dug deep within himself to find enough compassion for others. He decided to "stand up and lead as if we were going to survive [the] cold and outlast [the] last-gasp push"[3] required to survive the battle, win the war, and live free. In other words, he kept going because his brothers-in-arms needed him and depended on him.

There is something remarkably powerful that happens when men on a vital mission—a cause beyond themselves—band together to support one another in battle after battle. They often become *heroes*.

Don Malarkey stayed the course and returned to battle. In fact, no man in his company spent as much consecutive time on the front lines as he did.

Our friend Greg Johnson is an avid World War II buff and also our literary agent. He was privileged to go on a Band of Brothers tour to all the major European battlefields depicted in the HBO series produced by Tom Hanks and Steven Spielberg. Don Malarkey and his buddy Buck Compton—both in their late eighties—were also on the tour.

Greg recounted,

These old soldiers from the 101st Airborne were treated like heroes everywhere we went in Europe, especially in Belgium (Bastogne) and Holland. The young people had grown up hearing stories of how the American "angels from heaven" dropped from parachutes and dug foxholes around town to save their grandparents from the Nazis, and they treated Buck and Don like rock stars when they saw their military jackets. But the most emotional moment of the trip was accompanying the two men to an American cemetery in Luxembourg, where many of their comrades were buried. Don, ever the expressive Irishman, knelt at one white cross in a sea of white crosses—that of Alex Penkala, one of his best buddies from the war—and wept openly at the memories; at the thought that Alex, who died at the age of twenty-two, didn't get the chance to live a full life. Just as the sun was slipping down, young soldiers on duty at the cemetery honored these old war heroes and their fallen comrade by playing taps.

Later, when we walked through the Ardennes Forest with Don and Buck, among tall pine trees on a beautiful and peaceful summer day, you could still see the outline of many of the foxholes that barely sheltered the soldiers from the freezing cold and incoming enemy fire during those terrifying winter days from December 1944 to January 1945.

On the way home to America, on the airplane, I walked by Don and Buck, who were asleep in seats next to each other. Don was leaning on Buck's shoulder, and Buck's head was on Don's head—both of them sound asleep, sawing logs. And I smiled, realizing that these two men, in the twilight of their lives, were still the closest of brothers. How many months had they slept in close quarters in muddy, cold foxholes? Their bond was beyond friendship. It was the closest kind of brotherhood imaginable between men in a fight for a common cause, each one willing to give his life for the other.

What is a hero? A hero is an ordinary guy, with faults and flaws and fears and financial stresses, who signs up for a mission or cause that is greater than himself, committing to a band of brothers who will walk together through all kinds of battles in life—for the love of God and family and the good of humanity.

Not every hero finds himself in a war scenario as graphic and epic as World War II. But most men understand at a gut level that a war between good and evil is going on all around us and sometimes even within us. If justice and good are to emerge victorious, we can't do it alone. Even the Lone Ranger had Tonto. All the comic book superheroes have sidekicks and friends. The fictional Avengers combine each of their superpowers to make one superforce for good in the universe.

This is also how good men change the world. Each brings his talents to the stage of friendship and uses them together with the talents of others to create a team that can do mighty and marvelous things. When one man runs out of strength or loses courage, the others lift their companion to safety and fight enemies on his behalf until he can get back in the game.

David had his thirty-seven mighty men. Jesus had his twelve disciples. King Arthur had his various Knights of the Round Table. Frodo had his Company of the Ring (four hobbits, two men, one elf, one dwarf, and one wizard, to be exact). There is something about a band of brothers— friends who are on a quest or a journey together, working for a common cause—that universally appeals to the soul of a hero. We all want to belong to a tribe where we are known, valued, and loved—and missed when we aren't there. A man is at his best when he is part of an entourage that is helping the world and diminishing evil—whether that man is wearing a soldier's camouflage fatigues, a sweat suit, a business suit, or worn-out blue jeans. As the saying goes, not all heroes wear capes.

Men need good friends, the kind of friends they come to think of as brothers. We need them much more than we may realize.

One who has unreliable friends soon comes to ruin, but there is a friend who sticks closer than a brother.

PROVERBS 18:24, NIV

Male Friendships versus Female Friendships

Women sometimes believe that men don't have friends. Not so, says Geoffrey Greif, author of *Buddy System*, a research-heavy book about men in friendships. "Men don't have friendships in the way women define friendships," he writes. "Guys get together and have shoulder-to-shoulder relationships—we do things together, as compared with women, who are more apt to have face-to-face relationships."[4] Men show up at a sports bar to cheer on their team, side by side, observing a contest of might, mayhem, and testosterone. Women meet for lunch at a cute new French café; order something colorful, tiny, and tasty; and look at each other while they talk. And talk. And talk.

A full-on emotional conversation between women can give most men an overwhelmingly intense desire to escape to a ballgame, the golf course, or a quiet run in the country.

With exceptions, of course, men don't tend to meet up to chat. Conversation, in and of itself, is not usually considered a fun activity. In general, guys prefer to meet up for poker nights, eighteen holes of golf, or a couple of sweaty games of half-court basketball. They go rock climbing, camping, or mountain biking. Or they tinker with a car engine. The talking and sharing happens "by the way" or "on the way," as issues, questions, or opinions come to mind.

Even Christian men's groups made up of intellectually or spiritually curious sorts gather around the Bible or a book or an idea or a topic to explore and dissect—a focused activity they can discuss side by side. Women don't need a book or a topic to gather around; just put them in a room facing each other and they can fill it with hundreds of words and thoughts with seemingly no effort at all. And they love this. In fact, oxytocin, the happy hormone, increases in women after they have an evening of talking and sharing.

Not surprisingly, most men form their closest friendships when they are young, before the pressures of marriage, work, and fatherhood conspire to take up so much of their time. Friendships as a natural priority are reprised when men grow older, the nest empties, and they retire, giving them more time to spend with male friends. As a witness, go to any well-worn diner in America any morning of the week. You can nearly always spot a table of retired men in baseball caps, well into their second cup of coffee, shooting the breeze.

During the years from ages thirty to fifty, men have to be more intentional about staying in touch with other male friends, because it might not happen if they don't carve out time for it. The easiest way for most guys to do this is to meet up with a friend or two for a shared activity they all enjoy, a meaningful service project, or both.

If you can, take time off—even once or twice a year—to do a weekend or weeklong mission project as a group. Work on building a home or a church building for those in need, help at a medical clinic, or combine your gifts and talents to achieve whatever you can.

If you've ever gone on a short-term mission trip with a group to do something selfless for others, you've probably experienced one of the greatest highs of your life. The bonding, the satisfaction of working together, the feeling of accomplishment, the sense of God's grace, and the smiles on the faces of the people whose lives you made better are about as good as it gets this side of heaven.

I (Steve) experience these feelings whenever our New Life team hosts weekends of healing. The camaraderie in these settings is both meaningful and uplifting. To be part of a group that desires to help others gives me one of the best feelings I've ever had. It energizes and humbles me, amazes and inspires me. In short, it makes me feel like the man God created me to be.

As men we love to be part of something that requires our talents and efforts in a team setting. When something pushes us out of our comfort zone, we know we're not alone; we have a circle of guys who have our backs. Being part of a supportive team is transformative. And I can tell you this: Commitment to a group effort will keep you from being bored and will keep your mind so busy that it won't have time to sink into the pitfalls of sin and self-pity.

If you struggle with adrenaline-based addictions, you may find that being proactive in a team of brothers who work together to support others will help you stay sober and give you a bigger rush than any drug or temptation.

Not every male-bonding experience needs to be dramatic or life altering to add meaning to your life. Joining a sports league, having a regular tee time, going to a ballgame, co-coaching your kids' teams, or gathering at a sports-themed restaurant that has more TV screens than tables allows for easy, natural, and fun male bonding that will lift your spirits and bring out the best in you. Fishing, hunting, hiking, surfing, biking, rock climbing, or skiing (on snow or water) provides countless opportunities for men to bond while in their element. Something about being in nature, the whole "man versus wild" experience, creates a band of brothers experience that goes beyond the activity itself. These times can be enhanced and deepened by reaching out to fatherless teens or friends who are going through rough times and including them in your outing.

Men may approach friendship differently than women, but in terms of how they value those friendships, the research is clear: *Men care a great deal about their friends.*

> "If we use a women's paradigm for friendship, we're making a mistake," says Geoffrey Greif, a professor at the University of Maryland's School of Social Work, who has studied how 386 men made, kept, and nurtured friendships. Men might not be physically or emotionally expressive, he says, but we derive great support from our friendships.[5]

Most men would jump in to help a friend in need or in pain, like the heroes they are at heart. But they may show their caring in different ways. This is why men generally need a shared mission to bond deeply and create a truly close friendship. Because we are motivated by action and activity, our friendships grow best in shared efforts toward a common goal, and especially in overcoming challenges together. The popularity of team sports among men is no coincidence or accident. But don't miss this: That same male instinct can be harnessed by the Holy Spirit to accomplish amazing things in our world—to help others and leave a lasting legacy.

In the next chapter, we will discuss finding your mission, and we will share examples of how to gather other men around a shared vision and call to action. You will see that, with a small band of brothers, you can do heroic good deeds right where you work or live, even in the busiest times of life when you are raising kids and working hard to pay the bills.

Choose Your Team Wisely

The late Jim Rohn, a well-known motivational speaker and author, wrote about the importance of true friendship:

> Friendship is probably the greatest support system in the world, so don't deny yourself the time to develop it. Nothing can match it. It's extraordinary in its benefit.
>
> Friends are those wonderful people who know all about you and still like you. I lost one of my dearest friends when he was 53—heart attack. . . . I used to say that if I was stuck in a foreign jail somewhere accused unduly, and if they would allow me one phone call, I would call David. Why? He would come and get me. That's a real friend—somebody who would come and get you.[6]

Who is in your inner circle—the friend or friends who would come for you if you ended up in a foreign jail? Most of us don't have more than two or three friends like that. They are the ones you can call at midnight to meet you at the hospital if a loved one has been in an accident, and they will simply show up to be there with you. Guys like that are gold. You do not want to neglect those friend-ships. Send your friends a text or share a funny cartoon, a good quote, or a passage of Scripture when they come to mind. Ask how you can pray for them today. If they live nearby, make time for a regular coffee or breakfast date, or get together to watch a ballgame every couple of months. Planning regular times together will keep these prime relationships in good repair and add enormous meaning and fun to your life.

Studies show that the best indicator for having a long, happy, and fulfilled life is not nutrition or exercise—it is good, close relationships.[7] The hero's journey is not a solo trek. Be proactive about gathering your band of brothers, your superhero team.

Here are a few questions for you to ponder today as you contemplate your circle of friends:

Who are the five friends you spend the most time with?
Do they have the kind of qualities you'd like to see in
    your own life?
Can you see being friends with them into your old age?
What would it take for that to happen?
How can you strengthen and deepen the friendships
    you already have?
If you don't have a few close guy friends, what can you
    do to begin to connect and gather your own band of
    brothers?

Traits of Healthy Male Friendships

As you ponder these questions, look for male friends who have qualities that you know will bring out the best in you. Avoid friendships with men who will discourage you or lead you down paths you don't want to travel. What qualities matter most to you in a friend? Here are ten key traits we have observed in healthy and enjoyable male friendships. You may think of more, but these ten came to mind for us.

Loyalty

In *Same Kind of Different as Me*, the poignant bestselling book about a friendship between a homeless man and a businessman, there is a scene where Denver (the homeless man) notes that white people have a habit of going fishing just for the sport of it, calling it "catch and release." This puzzles him. Denver says to his friend, in one of the more moving scenes in the book, "If you is fishin for a friend you just gon' catch and release, then I ain't got no desire to be your friend. . . . But if you is lookin for a *real* friend, then I'll be one. Forever."[8]

Forever friends are rare treasures. If you have one, show him that you value and appreciate having him in your life. Once you make a loyal friend, commit to being there for him for the long haul, in good times and bad. You don't have to know what to say if your friend goes through a tragedy or a really bad time. You don't need to be a trained grief counselor. Go to the hospital where your friend's wife is having surgery, bringing with you a couple of tacos and his favorite soft drink. Listen to him and nod with compassion as you throw a fishing line into the lake on a camping trip. Ninety percent of life and friendship really is just being the person who checks in and shows up.

Vulnerable Honesty

In his vulnerable book titled *Scary Close*, about learning to drop the masks in relationships, Donald Miller discovers a great paradox of friendship: "We don't think of our flaws as the glue that binds us to the people we love, but they are. Grace only sticks to our imperfections. Those who can't accept their imperfections can't accept grace either."[9]

Another author, Heather Kopp, who spent years trying to mask her alcoholism, discovered a closeness in her recovery group that had somehow escaped her in Christian circles. After many months, she observed that "people bond more deeply over shared brokenness than they do over shared beliefs."[10] What a profound insight. In a follow-up article in the *HuffPost*, Kopp observed that when people bond over beliefs, the unspoken value of the group, achieved through agreement, is being right. But when people gather with a goal to heal, the shared value, achieved through honesty, is being real.[11] This invites true community if it is done in an atmosphere of safety and acceptance. If you want true friendship, drop the idea that you have to impress other people or be right about every issue. Be honest. Be real. Be yourself.

Humor and Fun

Few things relax us and make friendship more enjoyable than sharing funny observations and laughing at ourselves.

I (Dave) share a love of laughter with Steve, and it's actually kind of funny how we began working together. We both had a passion for the recovery movement, and we both worked in Christian counseling (at separate businesses). Decades ago, Steve and I met at the church we both attended, when he was in the music ministry and I was in the teaching ministry. In our discussions about recovery, I suggested that Steve teach a class called "The Person Sitting Next to You Could Be an Alcoholic." He agreed, and it proved to be a surprising success. The experience seemed to light a fire under both of us, because we independently began mulling over how to better minister to those in recovery in the body of Christ.

Without knowing what the other was doing, we each submitted a book proposal to the same publisher (but to different acquisition editors) for the concept of creating a Bible with notes, testimonies, and stories specifically for those in recovery from addiction, correlating scriptural truths with the Twelve Steps of Alcoholics Anonymous. In a comedy of errors, both editors brought our proposals to the same publication-committee meeting, and it was only then that they realized two different authors were pitching the same basic concept. We ended up as coauthors on what became *The Life Recovery Bible*, published by Tyndale House, which has blessed millions of people. The finished product was so much better than what either of us could have accomplished alone, in large part due to our growing friendship and collaboration.

We joke that the reason our friendship has lasted so long through so many shared endeavors (writing, speaking, on-air counseling) is that we both know and regularly practice the Twelve Steps with each other.

It is one of the blessings of old friends that you can afford to be stupid with them.

RALPH WALDO EMERSON

Positive Attitude and Encouragement

As we've shared before, we have found that almost every man is starving for a little encouragement and positive input. But guys will rarely express their deep need for assurance and validation. Men's friendships deepen when they become each other's number one fans. In the words of noted author Ken Blanchard, "Catch people doing something right."[12] Affirm their efforts—early and often—because the world, and sometimes our own negative voice, is shouting our inadequacies.

In the book of Acts, we read that the apostles had a friend whom they nicknamed Barnabas, which means "Son of Encouragement,"[13] because he had a knack for doing and saying things that lifted others up in some way. We all need a Barnabas in our lives, and we need to be a Barnabas for someone else.

In Paul's letter to the church at Thessalonica, he advises them to "encourage each other and build each other up."[14] Recently I (Dave) heard someone say that the word *encourage* literally means to put courage into someone—to strengthen and fill with purpose. How? Through our belief in the person and our positive, uplifting words. Men help each other to be braver and better than we would be alone.

Sharing and Listening

We have all been around the kind of guy who hogs the limelight and talks so much that it ruins the opportunity for anyone else to be seen or heard. Guys like that are perpetually onstage, auditioning for who knows what, trying to impress others.

On the other hand, there are guys who never share beyond the depth of "How 'bout them Cowboys?" No doubt you've had the awkward experience of being with someone who gives one- or two-word answers to all your questions.

A good friendship is like Ping-Pong—the conversational

ball is batted back and forth in fairly equal measure. It is a rare skill to know how to ask good questions, listen deeply, and ask good follow-up questions. Guys who master this skill tend to attract and keep good friends. At some level, everybody wants to be *heard*.

If being a good conversationalist and listener doesn't come naturally to you, make it a goal to learn how to converse well in the same way you would learn any other skill. There are lots of books and online videos on the topic of communication. Make sure you don't just learn how to speak in an interesting way; also study and practice how to *listen* so that others will enjoy sharing with you and feel deeply heard. Active listening is a skill that can be taught and learned. A good rule of thumb is to try to speak and listen (and ask good questions) in equal measure. Seek out and build friendships with guys who do the same.

Though Steve and I are both public speakers (and born *talkers*), we have had to learn to listen actively and attentively, both in a counseling setting and to those who call in for advice on our New Life radio program. To be honest, we have both had to learn how to listen more deeply to our wives and kids, and we both sought out help and advice from professional therapists when we realized, at various points in our lives, that our loved ones were not feeling truly seen and heard by us.

James 5:16 tells us to confess our sins to each other, and the impact of doing so can be tremendously healing. Long ago, I (Steve) made a commitment that I would inform someone of anything that was troubling me or tempting me or tripping me up. That someone has always been Dave. I often wonder what he thinks when he sees my number on his cell phone. When we talk, the burden of silent struggle is lifted, and I am always enlightened and encouraged. Everyone needs a Dave. Such friendships are invaluable.

> *When someone deeply listens to you, it is like holding out*
> *a dented cup you've had since childhood and watching it*
> *fill up with fresh, cold water.*
>
> JOHN FOX, "WHEN SOMEONE DEEPLY LISTENS TO YOU"

Soul Connection

You may have heard the phrase *mo anam cara*, which is a Gaelic term that means "my soul friend." A soul friend is someone with whom you can be completely honest. In a soul friend's presence, you feel heard and understood. You trust each other, respect each other, and share a spiritual bond. You show up in moments big and small, joyous and sorrowful. Not every friend will be a soul friend—not by a long shot. But it is a worthy goal to cultivate at least one soul friendship in the journey of life.

The movie *Tolkien*, about the author J. R. R. Tolkien's coming of age before and during World War I, is an awesome study on the friendships of men. Perhaps no two circumstances create male soul friends more easily than scholastic camaraderie and going to war together. There is a fictionalized scene in the film, set during Tolkien's college years, where he gets completely blotto after discovering that the girl he loves is engaged to another man. He ends up in the yard that night, yelling nonsense at the windows of the university housing units above him.

Geoffrey Bache Smith, one of his more empathetic and kindhearted pals, goes out in the night to check on him. Though these English chaps were usually stoic, sharp witted, and manly in their normal lives, Tolkien's heart is broken beyond his ability to hold it together at this point. He apologizes to Geoffrey and says, "I'm sorry. I'm in a bit of a mess." Then he starts to weep. His friend puts his arms around his devastated, drunken buddy and says, "It's okay. It's okay. That's okay. I've got you. I've got you."[15]

As iron sharpens iron, so a friend sharpens a friend.

PROVERBS 27:17

As it happens, the two friends end up as soldiers in that terrible war of the trenches, World War I. As depicted in the movie, Tolkien risks his life to try to find his brother-in-arms. The eventual word of Geoffrey's death is a dagger to his heart, but their soul friendship colors Tolkien's heart and his writings for the rest of his life. Their friendship, along with that of two other close buddies, forever deepens Tolkien's experience of life's shared joys and woes. The brotherly bonds of male soul friendship are echoed in all of Tolkien's Lord of the Rings books, which have touched and encouraged so many.

Mutual Interests and Curiosity

C. S. Lewis wrote in his classic book *The Four Loves*, "People who bore one another should meet seldom; people who interest one another, often."[16] A friend who is curious and always learning something new in a category of life that interests you will inspire you to do the same. You'll naturally want to make time for such friends in your life.

Determine to be an interesting person by remaining curious and open to learning new skills, perspectives, and ideas, and you will bring so much depth to all your friendships. In our profession, we have endless opportunities to sharpen our career skills through seminars and conventions, workshops and classes. Take advantage of your shared interests and go with a friend to an event that will nurture your shared hobby, career skills, or other interests.

Do you and a buddy love to fish? During the winter months, attend a class together on how to tie fishing flies. Go to a weekend men's retreat or a men's Bible study with a friend to deepen your spiritual connections. Attend an antique car show with a fellow car buff. Go to hear a veteran, a mountain climber, or a Civil War expert give a talk. Attend a local lecture or a book-signing event by a favorite author.

Go to a wood-carving class. Whatever your shared interest, there is an event that can encourage you and teach you new and interesting information. And of course you can stay in touch by sharing good videos, books, podcasts, articles, or quotes you each come across. Dave and I often share interesting articles and the latest research and creative ideas on recovery from addiction and inner healing, as this has long been a shared interest and passion of ours.

Shared Adventures

What do you love to do just for the sheer challenge or fun of it? Growing and sustaining a friendship with someone who shares that passion should be easy. How many friendships and business relationships have been forged on a golf course, while rock climbing, or during long-distance bike rides? What activity do you really enjoy that would be enhanced by the company of a few good men?

Our friend Jake is from Colorado. During the week he works as an EMT, which is an adventure of its own. But on the weekends, he and his good buddy Trevor have set a mutual goal to climb all fifty-three of the major Rocky Mountain peaks that reach above fourteen thousand feet— the so-called Fourteeners.[17] The two men have almost reached their goal! This shared activity challenges them, gives them opportunities to talk and encourage each other, builds stamina and physical strength, and gets them out in nature. Jake shared that when he is bored, his mind tends to wander into troublesome areas—he can easily fall into addictive behaviors or temptations or succumb to negative and depressive thoughts. Both his friendship with Trevor and their shared Fourteener goal connect him to the best part of himself—the soul of the hero within. He feels healthy in body, mind, and soul.

Confidentiality

If you and your friend are going to be honest with each other, you must be able to keep strict confidences. You should be able to ask a good friend not to repeat something personal and trust that he will keep your confidence, and vice versa. Treat this information as a treasure to be guarded.

The reason Alcoholics Anonymous works so well is that there is a cone of safety in their meetings. Everyone pledges that whatever is shared in the meeting stays there and will not be repeated outside the group. If Christian brothers would follow this format, many more men could openly talk about their struggles and get the empathy, support, and help they need.

Scheduled Time

It can be frustrating to befriend someone who is so crazy busy that he doesn't have time or make time for you. If you are new in town, it might be easy to find another guy who is also a new arrival, or new to the office or church, because his friendship card isn't already fully punched with lots of established friends. Be creative and accommodating in order to respect his time. Perhaps volunteer to go to one of his kids' baseball games, or help him fix his car if you're gifted that way. Ask him to help you rake leaves and enjoy a cup of coffee around the fire afterward. Because time is such a valuable commodity, try to get double duty out of your time together: Check something off your to-do list while also connecting with your friend. No matter how busy you are, carve out some time each month to stay in touch and do something enjoyable with a guy friend—or two or three.

* * *

When it comes to being the best man you can be, there are few things as vital to the hero's journey as the friends you choose to travel with you. Sometimes you will find brotherhood in surprising ways and surprising places.

Bands of Brothers in Unlikely Places

I (Steve) want to end this chapter with a story about the way one man, a leader at one of our retreat/healing weekends for teens, used some of the techniques in this chapter to create a unique Band of Brothers experience that transformed a young man's life.

As the teaching pastor of Northview Church in Carmel, Indiana, I am amazed by the level of ministry that happens in the congregation. I continually see examples of people who know how to love others as Jesus loves us—often in dramatic, creative, and natural ways. It blesses my heart to see such a healthy ministry based on inclusion and love. Nobody is left out in the cold. All are welcomed into the circle of Christ's love.

Our church holds an occasional experience called the Discipleship Walk, where for one weekend, followers of Christ shower the love of Jesus on one another in healing and profound ways. I attended one of the weekends for men, and let me just say, it was a TNT experience for me. (Not TNT as in dynamite, but TNT as in "tears 'n' tissue.") I was so moved by the love expressed by other men—to me and to each other—that I was dripping tears like a leaky faucet, off and on, all weekend.

Our church provides the same experience for teenagers. The results of a weekend of face-to-face interaction, sharing, and hugs—without phones or screens or technology of any kind—is quite astounding. A young man, age sixteen, arrived at the event dressed in black from head to toe. I'm talking black clothes, shoe-polish black hair, black eye makeup, and black-painted fingernails. As you can imagine, he did not blend in.

On the first afternoon, everyone gathered in groups to meet their leader for the weekend. A young or inexperienced leader might not have had a clue how to handle a goth teen on a "Christian discipleship" weekend. But the forty-two-year-old leader knew a lot about teenagers and what was behind the whole goth perspective. He knew that this kid had found a place of acceptance in an alternative community that thrived on being different. The leader introduced himself, and then others around the table started introducing themselves. The goth teen didn't volunteer anything more than a quiet hello.

The wise and compassionate leader looked the young man in the eye, smiled, and initiated a conversation.

"I see that you have black fingernails. Do a lot of your friends paint their fingernails black?"

"Yes," came the muffled reply.

"If you happened to pack some black nail polish, I sure would like for you to paint my nails. That way we would have something in common, other than the fact that we both probably feel a bit awkward being males in this society."

"Later?" came the one-word question.

"No, not later. There is nothing more important than you and me having something in common. We should start with something now. So if you want to go get that polish, I'm ready to 'nail' down our friendship." The goth boy smiled and left the room, returning a few minutes later with a bottle of ink-black nail polish.

After the leader had his nails painted black, he encouraged everyone else in the group to get their nails painted as well—a show of community and solidarity. In other words, they created an instant Band of Brothers—or, you might say, Men in Black.

I probably don't need to spell out the rest of the story. You can guess. It was the beginning of a transformation for that young man—and for some other guys in the group as well, who learned an important lesson about acceptance.

When I heard the story, I was overcome with emotion. Little had I known there was a man in my church who got the "loving like Jesus does" thing exactly right. This group leader is a hero in my eyes. More important, he's a hero in the eyes of a young man who never expected to see that level of love and acceptance.

There is a classic little poem, written in the early 1900s by Edwin Markham, called "Outwitted." Perhaps you've heard it:

> He drew a circle that shut me out—
> Heretic, rebel, a thing to flout.
> But Love and I had the wit to win:
> We drew a circle that took him in! [18]

You never know where a fellowship of unlikely heroes might be found. King David's famous mighty men started out as quite a motley crew of unlikely characters. Here's how his band of not-so-merry men are described in 1 Samuel 22:2: "Everyone who was in distress, and everyone who was in debt, and everyone who was bitter in soul, gathered to him. And he became commander over them."[19]

This verse always makes us laugh out loud. Anyone in long-term ministry has probably looked around in a moment of feeling overwhelmed and wondered whether everyone who comes to them is depressed, in debt, or discontented.

In David's case, the numbers eventually swelled to *four hundred* men. But the wonder of the gospel is that God puts his power into frail, needy, messed-up human vessels. And when we join together under God's influence and leadership, miracles happen.

When depressed, indebted, and discontented guys experience a sense of belonging in the body of Christ, they may also discover their true value as made in the image of God, then commit themselves to the pathway of healing and restoration. Men who find their identity in Jesus and feel they are part of a vital mission can quickly turn into mighty men, a band of brothers, a fellowship of friends. Men who discover the hero within their own soul and join up with other like-minded guys to do good and spread the love of God in this world are *unstoppable*.

Proactively and purposefully, find or gather your own tribe, clan, fellow warriors, Inklings, Hobbits, or unlikely but willing mighty men. Then submit yourselves to the leadership of Jesus Christ and watch your masculine souls come alive.

5

YOUR MISSION, SHOULD YOU CHOOSE TO ACCEPT IT

Heroic Secret #5: Find Your Earthly Purpose

If you can't figure out your purpose, figure out your passion.
For your passion will lead you right into your purpose.

T. D. JAKES

Maybe you're younger than we are and don't remember gathering in the living room around the TV on Sunday nights, anticipating the heart-pounding theme music that opened *Mission Impossible*, the hit TV show of the 1960s.

Each episode started the same way: A spy named Jim Phelps discovered a reel-to-reel tape recorder (spying was a bulkier profession back then) with a message in a deep voice stating the details of his latest mission. Every message ended with the same call to action: "Your mission, should you choose to accept it . . ."

Then the tape would self-destruct in a foggy puff of smoke.

By the time Tom Cruise introduced the character of Ethan Hunt in the movies based on the TV show, the spy business was much leaner and snazzier and even more exciting. But the anticipation of the mission was the same. Hunt would never know what his orders might be or where they would take him. He only knew there would be travel, danger, intrigue, fast cars, speedboats, bad guys with guns, and a beautiful female spy somewhere along the way to saving the world. And if he or anyone on his IMF team were captured or killed, he was told, "The Secretary will disavow any knowledge of your actions."

Obviously such movies are custom-made for men. The scripts come from the fertile ferment of testosterone-fueled minds, and the filmmakers have sold millions of dollars' worth of tickets by targeting every man who has ever dreamed of being a hero who rescues the universe from evil while wearing a well-made Italian suit (that never gets torn or singed or wrinkled).

Besides all the cool gadgets, what makes these heroic spy adventures so compelling is the hero's willingness to tackle whatever surprise mission comes his way from the powers that be. We don't recall ever seeing a superspy listening to his mission and then yawning and saying, "You know what? No, I'm not going to accept this one. I'm going to a Toledo Mud Hens preseason game. But hey, thanks for the offer!"

You probably know where we're going with this, don't you?

Men become heroes by saying *yes* to exciting missions. And let's face it: A hero without a mission, or a hero who always says *no* to missions, is no superspy.

It's all about the mission, guys. So let's dig deeper and explore ways you can discover your particular calling, mission, or purpose on earth.

And then, of course, this chapter will self-destruct.

What's Your Earthly Purpose?

We hear a lot about mission these days in various leadership conferences: Being "on mission" for or with God. Finding your calling. Realizing your purpose.

But what does it mean exactly to be *on mission*? More important, what does it mean for *you* and your one unique life?

First, we believe each of us has an overarching life mission—what we often call a *life goal* or *purpose*. An example of this might be the first response in the well-known Westminster Shorter Catechism, written in 1647: "Man's chief end is to glorify God and to enjoy him forever." Not a bad life mission to adopt. Another example might be "to bring a little more of heaven down to earth."

The Bible tells us that Jesus "grew in wisdom and in stature and in favor with God and all the people."[1] That's a wonderful life goal.

Much has been written in the last decade about "living incarnationally," which is an idea derived from the way Jesus came to earth to represent and live out God's love in ways we could see, touch, hear, and understand. Perhaps your overarching mission is to be a living example of Jesus' teachings in the world and to share the gospel in word and deed. Or it could be as straightforward as fully experiencing the life God has given you and using every opportunity to grow in faith and glorify him.

Pray about and seek a life mission that resonates within your own heart—one that inspires and focuses you, that aligns your goals with God's purposes. As Rick Warren wrote in his bestselling book *The Purpose Driven Life*, "Without God, life has no purpose, and without purpose, life has no meaning. Without meaning, life has no significance or hope."[2] Every so often in life, we need to pause and ask ourselves,

Where am I heading?

Why am I doing what I'm doing?
Is God at the helm of this goal?

Once you find an overall life-mission statement, write it down and post it someplace where you will see it often. As you grow in faith and experience life's realities, keep it in front of you as a way to focus and stay on the hero path, as a way to remember and stay committed to your highest purpose.

Second, identify your more specific life mission, the one that is unique to you and your giftings—or, as we like to call them, your *superpowers.*

Albert Schweitzer was awarded the Nobel Peace Prize in 1952 for his medical missionary work in saving African communities from malaria and other diseases. He was inspired by the life and sacrifice of Jesus and "found that his life of helping others provided him with a far deeper sense of personal meaning and satisfaction than he had ever experienced."[3] In speaking to students, Schweitzer often gave a bit of advice: "I do not know your destiny, but I do know one thing: the only ones of you who will be truly happy are those who have sought and found how to serve."[4]

In a quote often attributed to others—including Aristotle and Albert Schweitzer—Marcus Bach, a longtime professor at the University of Iowa School of Religion, articulated his view of God's calling on our lives: "You'll discover that the place where your talent meets the world's needs is the job God has in mind for you."[5] Frederick Buechner, the prolific author and theologian, put it this way: "The place God calls you to is the place where your deep gladness and the world's deep hunger meet."[6]

A great place to begin mulling over your specific mission or calling is to ask yourself, *What brings me deep gladness? What makes me feel alive?* Then look to see where the world is hurting, what the world is hungering for or delighted by, and see what you can uniquely contribute. "The world" could mean the world at your doorstep, the world in the office hallway, the world in your community, or the world at large.

Part of this process will be discovering or honing your "superpowers"— talents, abilities, or gifts that come easily to you, that fill you with joy and renewed passion for life, and that bless others in some way. Quite often when we are using our superpowers, we experience a state of flow where time seems to disappear and we are fully involved in the present. Think about activities you engage in that make you lose track of time. This could provide a clue to your natural bent, your God-infused superpower.

Another way to uncover your giftedness is to ask yourself, *What do I tend to remember without much effort? Where do I have incredible recall?* You may forget the name of a person you just met, but you have almost photographic recall of . . . what? Recently our friend Josh, a professional writer and speaker, shared one of his superpowers with us:

> I tend to be forgetful by nature. I lose my car keys and reading glasses with aggravating regularity. But when I hear or read a quote that I love, my brain just

remembers it, word for word. Automatically. Great quotes are like Velcro in my brain. Remembering quotes is one of my weird talents. But it makes sense because I love a well-written phrase, I like the sound of words, and I get a kick out of stringing thoughts together in meaningful or witty ways that encourage others. So they stick with me.

Maybe you have a mind for numbers. Maybe you remember sports statistics easily. Maybe you see a business plan and find yourself itching to start reorganizing and structuring and putting it all together in a way that will appeal to investors. Or maybe you have a knack for taking apart an engine and putting it back together. For you, remembering where all the parts go is a no-brainer. Maybe you see a newly constructed building and immediately begin to see how landscaping could be used to accentuate its best features. Or when you hear a song on the radio, your mind remembers it with ease, and you can play it on your guitar later with no problem. Maybe you memorize movie lines without trying. Whatever it is that your mind does with ease—whether it involves memory, analysis, synthesis, or creativity—these skills often hint at your innate gifts or talents, because they serve or support "that thing you do."

Not long ago, we were chatting with a friend who is amazing at accounting and keeping track of his clients' financial records. He remembers numbers and statistics, financial projections, and monies receivable and payable—all without opening a file. We joke that if you were to put a cartoon bubble above his head, it would look like an Excel spreadsheet. Not surprisingly, when he was a kid, he was obsessed with collecting things, counting them, and putting them in order. He had a knack for searching and finding items of value to him, but the great fun was in counting, recording, and organizing his finds. When he was cataloguing his collections, he said, time ceased to exist. He was in the zone. These boyhood skills, which revealed his natural bent, later morphed and grew into his adult vocation as a super accountant. Your childhood hobbies may hint at your adult superpowers, your God-given talents.

What would you choose to do just because it's fun and makes you feel alive and focused and lost in the moment? For me (Steve), I'm often happiest when I'm lost in thought, coming up with new ideas for our ministry, a new book, a talk, or a seminar. I get lost in the world of ideas and creative ways to help others—in the same way my friend gets lost in his columns of numbers. My mind is like a popcorn popper, exploding with catchy or helpful or innovative ideas. I love coming up with titles and themes. I might have been good at advertising if I hadn't pursued counseling and vocational ministry. Not every idea is a great one, of course. Some only sound brilliant at 2:00 a.m. when I can't sleep, but they fall by the wayside when seen in the sane light of day. One such idea was a slogan I came up with for New Life: "We Love Hurting People." My team had to point out that this could be taken two very different ways.

Some of the wild ideas that came to me as I walked or prayed or doodled on a napkin or brainstormed with other creative folks led to ministries such as the Women of Faith conferences, the book *Toxic Faith*, life-altering Healing Is a Choice workshops, and dozens of topics and seminars that have borne good fruit and blessed millions of people. This may sound like boasting or bragging, but I don't believe it is. I'm convinced that God wired me with a creative mind and that the Holy Spirit inspired these ideas that I certainly could not have come up with on my own. Moreover, the collaborative creativity that came from others to turn these ideas into tangible events is far beyond anything I could have accomplished otherwise.

Working on a live call-in radio show is also a blessing for me. When someone asks me a question, my mind starts popping with information, memories, ideas, quotes, bits of Scripture, advice, and stories that are somehow funneled and focused into the answers I give on the air. As a public speaker who often has to speak off the cuff, I have endless material to draw upon from the "idea machine" working overtime in my brain.

My overarching mission and purpose in life is to glorify God, love well, and help others heal. My superpower combines creative energy with a love for words, music, painting or drawing, theater and drama. Sometimes I use my creativity for the sheer pleasure of it: Doodling a funny drawing for my kids. Dancing with my beautiful wife. Singing (like Sinatra of course) in the car on the way to work. But my calling is to communicate God's love and healing paths in innovative and memorable ways by pairing my creative abilities with my heart's desire to help others heal and grow.

I hope that by sharing my own "superpowers" I have succeeded in setting your mind to boil with ideas and insights about your own unique wiring from God, your own unique purpose. This might be an opportune moment to set this book aside and do a little personal reflecting with paper and pen—or whatever medium works best for you. What is your overall mission and purpose in life? What are some of your superpowers—those gifts that come easily to you but may not come as easily to others? Perhaps it's something you remember with ease or something you enjoyed doing when you were a kid. What activity brings you joy? How does this activity help or lift others up in some way? Where could your deep gladness meet a hunger in the world?

You may be wondering whether your unique mission is "spiritual enough." This is an unfortunate by-product of our tendency as Christians to fragment our lives into compartments. But in God's economy, there is no separation between *sacred* and *secular*. When we come into relationship with Jesus Christ and submit ourselves to his will and his guidance, *all of life* becomes set apart for God's glory and honor. *Everything* we do for the glory of God is by definition *sacred*. Many of the most spiritual men that Dave and I know, guys who are doing the most profound ministry, are meeting the world's needs in so-called secular settings. But by the power of the Holy Spirit, with great love and contagious enthusiasm, they are redeeming and sanctifying the world where they live.

"Whatever you do, work heartily, as for the Lord and not for men, knowing that from the Lord you will receive the inheritance as your reward."[7] We reflect God's image anytime we do something in service to him.

If we believe, as the apostle Paul says in Acts 17:28, that in God "we live and move and have our being,"[8] then using our gifts and talents in everyday life is holy.

In the heart of every man is a desperate desire for a battle to fight, an adventure to live, and a beauty to rescue.

JOHN ELDREDGE

There was a monk who spent his life in poverty, much of it in the kitchen among the pots and pans. Not exactly the tools of a hero's trade, you might think. But people were drawn to Brother Lawrence, to his humility and quiet joy and calm. They'd seek him out for advice and comfort and spiritual encouragement. In the classic book *The Practice of the Presence of God*, he says, "We ought not to be weary of doing little things for the love of GOD, for He regards not the greatness of the work, but the love with which it is performed."[9] The tasks may be small or big, impressive or mundane. Brother Lawrence realized that if we choose to live our lives with love and reverence for God, our deeds will matter in the heavenly realm even if no one on earth ever notices. Whether you are washing pots and pans, sweeping a floor, reconciling columns of numbers, climbing a mountain, or preaching a sermon to thousands, if you do it with an awareness of God's presence, if you do it for the love of God, you have tapped into your inner hero. You are doing your part, however small it may seem, to bring a bit more of heaven to earth.

Adventures Aren't Just for Superheroes

Now we'd like to get a bit more practical. What does doing everything "as for the Lord" look like in everyday life? We like to start each morning with a prayer that focuses our hearts and minds on God's presence and invites him to guide us during the day. Usually it's some variation of "Surprise me, God! I'm available to be used by you to bless someone else today."

Praying this way every morning helps us live each day with an awareness of God's power and purpose. It attunes us to whatever mission he might have for us that day, as if we are his secret agents to a waiting world. Praying, "Surprise me, God" means we are open and ready for random encounters that God ordains. When Jesus talked about having eyes to see and ears to hear, he was asking us to view the world and our own lives with spiritually enriched senses. When we have eyes to see and ears to hear, we become more aware of the Holy Spirit at work and how we might join him in serving people and bringing glory to God in whatever circumstances pop up during the day.

To illustrate how God can use us in the midst of our busy day-to-day lives, we want to introduce you to an ordinary guy in his late thirties who is finding ways to follow after God by using his own unique talents in ways that bless others.

Our friend Zeke is an active, in-demand architect and CEO of his own company, a loving husband, the father of two growing boys, and a man with a heart for adventure and a deep love for God, others, and the great outdoors. Zeke has a talent for design, construction, and building—skills he learned from working alongside his dad on various projects over the years. He eventually got his master's degree in architecture and today is one of the top architects in Colorado. He and his wife, Amy, live in the mountains in a home they designed, along with their boys and a variety of animals: goats, turkeys, sheep, dogs, cats, and the occasional visiting deer, mountain lion, or bear. They are as active as they can be in their local church and community.

Let's just say that life is full to the brim.

One of the ongoing conversations Zeke has with God goes like this: "How can I use my work as an architect to bring in more than an income? How can I use my vocation to be a blessing to others? What ideas do you have for me, God?" Then Zeke listens and ponders and prays as he waits for God to open doors and show him what to do.

We sat with Zeke in a comfortable booth in a Western-style restaurant in Golden, Colorado, and over mugs of black coffee, he told us how he runs his company, Root Architecture, as a professional architect and as a follower of Jesus. He described how he has been able to keep the heroic soul journey with God alive in the middle of a crazy busy life.

"I'm particular about how I operate my business," Zeke said, rubbing his neatly trimmed beard thoughtfully as he warmed to the subject. "I'm professional, a bit of a perfectionist, and I always want to do the best work possible for our clients. Of course, I need to make enough money to support my family and pay our employees, but even more so I want our company to be profitable, because the more profitable we are, the more impact we can have in doing good for those who need extra help."

Zeke paused and took a sip of coffee before continuing. "But let me tell you something I realized when we were just starting this business in its most fledgling state: You can't wait until you're making enough money to do something good for others. You can't say, 'When I make it big, then I'll do something extra for others.' So I did my best to make generosity a part of my company's DNA from the start."

Where did Zeke get the idea to make generosity a part of his company's mission, even as he was still working to get the business off the ground?

"Remember the biblical story of the widow who gave her two little pennies to God?" Zeke continued. "She didn't have much, but she gave what she had.[10] We tend to think that when we become the next Bill Gates, we can do great things to serve the world. But I believe the world needs more penny droppers than billionaires—men and women who are willing to do what they can and give what they can right where they are.

"Let me give you an example of how our company did what we could with the 'pennies' we had at the time. To make ends meet, we were doing a boatload of hands-on building projects back then, along with our architectural design. I had long admired the mission of Habitat for Humanity, and if we could have afforded it, I would have loved to build a dream house for a needy family. Unfortunately, that was way beyond our finances and available time. But the dream was still there, so I prayed about it. And an idea came to me. We could build a playhouse—a tree house—for a child who deserved something special after going through a difficult challenge. It wouldn't be an entire house for a family, but it would be using our pennies and time for something doable."

The idea took root in Zeke's imagination. He put out some inquiries and came across the story of a little girl, age six, who had been through some very rough spinal surgeries. Zeke proposed that his company build a fancy custom tree house for little Keira—a project he believed could be completed in a single day. He met with Keira's family and made sure she could take part in designing it. She asked for a castle tree house, and Zeke went to work on a design.

"The surprising thing," Zeke said, "was how excited people were to help once I decided to do the project. Folks want to be generous and do good; they just need someone to come up with an idea, turn it into a plan, take the lead, and make it happen. Once I started sharing about the project, subcontractors volunteered time on a Saturday to help build it. Vendors we'd worked with on other projects happily donated materials. Neighbors donated some logs we needed as support beams. Even my family got in on it. Several members donated money, my wife and kids joined in to give a hand with the finishing touches, my brother and sister-in-law spent all day working with the crew, and my mom—who loves to cook—brought lunch for the volunteers. The blessing of receiving was multiplied by the blessing each participant had in giving."

Keira loved her castle-style tree house, the family was deeply touched, and everyone received the blessing of working together to give something back.

"What I learned in that small, first project," Zeke said, "was that people are generous, and they want to contribute in ways that flow with their giftedness. It can be overwhelming when you look at all the needs of all the people on earth and then look at your own life that is so busy and so limited in finances. It's easy to get discouraged and do nothing. You may have heard the story of the guy who was walking along the beach and saw hundreds and hundreds of starfish that had washed up on shore during high tide. He started throwing some of them back into the ocean, where they could survive. Someone observed this and said, 'Hey, man, there is no way you can save all these starfish. There are too many. What difference are you making?' The guy picked up another starfish, threw it in the ocean, and said, 'Well, I just made a difference for that one.' Start with one starfish. Do what you can."

Zeke continued, "Most guys don't want to just do a job. They want to make a difference and have some meaning behind whatever task they do to earn a living. I think it starts with letting God's Word soak into your life so that it becomes a part of your personal DNA, so that generosity becomes a natural way to live in a world that is more and more self-focused. I read Scripture; listen to uplifting sermons, talks, and inspiring music; and try to spend time hiking and praying in the beauty of nature. I try to feed my own soul first. Then I try to be open each day to whatever surprises may come my way, and I tell God I'm willing to go wherever he opens an obvious door. It's a meaningful and adventurous way to live.

"A couple years ago, I went on a short-term mission with MANNA Worldwide to help serve in a feeding center for orphans in Guatemala. This one event opened doors that led to our hiring two architects from Central America to work for our company. Another time we were able to donate the architectural plans for a new building to house Mango Tree Coffee in Englewood, Colorado. It is a fresh, modern-designed, high-quality coffee shop where all the proceeds go to help impoverished children with nutrition, education, medical needs, and more. It's fun to see God open one door that leads to another and then another."

Zeke's enthusiasm was contagious. We could see clearly that this willingness to see and hear and follow God's leading put the "aroma and caffeine" in the ever-brewing imagination and mission of this young man's life.

Just then, Zeke's phone buzzed to life: A text. A client. He would have to be off soon, but he wanted to share one last thought.

"Life is a journey with unfolding paths and opening doors," he said. "And I always have the sense that God is at work, that he is on this journey with me. He is using my unique abilities and things I naturally love to do to both support my family and employees, and also to do something for people who need extra help—who are living in poverty, who have the challenge of illness, or who've been hit by bad news. God is the ultimate hero of my story, and I'm just his sidekick, joining him in the next adventure. Some days it feels kind of amazing and huge and awe-inspiring. Most days it feels like just showing up and being faithful and open and curious. But there is always this question buzzing in my heart: *I wonder what adventure God is brewing up today?*"

God, who said, "Let light shine out of darkness," has shone in our hearts. . . . But we have this treasure in jars of clay, to show that the surpassing power belongs to God and not to us.

2 CORINTHIANS 4:6-7, ESV

We hope you have caught a glimpse of the excitement you can have by allowing God to use you and your gifts as vessels for a mission or missions that are bigger than you. One of the greatest feelings in life is discovering and resting in your true identity, then finding and operating in your God-given, superpowerful gifting. Another is watching and praying for your daily missions to arrive and unfold, and then completing them!

Once you get into the habit of living this way, you will be forever ruined for living an ordinary life.

6

BEING A REAL MAN IN #METOO TIMES

Heroic Secret #6: Love and Respect Her Heart

*It is by standing up for the rights of girls and women
that we truly measure up as men.*

DESMOND TUTU

(Steve) have never met a man who, up front or down deep inside, did not want to be a hero to the woman he loves. It is a natural male inclination. But what we often don't consider is that women are heroes in their own right—especially when you consider the female heroes of the faith. These mighty women of the Bible were anything but helpless or needy. Let's take time to look at a few strong and inspiring women of faith.

First, I think of Esther. Esther knew that King Ahasuerus had unknowingly agreed to an evil, anti-Semitic plot that would kill every Jew in Persia. Rather than play it safe in the palace (where no one knew she was Jewish), Esther courageously and brilliantly laid out a plan that included a request for an audience before the king with the evil villain Haman present. She risked her life and intervened on behalf of her people, saving them from certain death. She was the ultimate hero of the Jewish people at vital and dangerous crossroads in history.[1]

Deborah served as a judge in Israel and was one of only five female prophets mentioned in the Old Testament.[2] She was known for her wisdom in settling disputes and also showed a talent for songwriting. Deborah summoned Barak, a war hero, and told him that God was commanding him to rise up and defeat Sisera, commander of the armies of Jabin, an evil king in Canaan who was oppressing the Israelites. The odds against them were overwhelming. Sisera had nine hundred iron chariots and thousands of foot soldiers at his command. Barak agreed to go to battle, but only if Deborah would go with him. She had already prophesied victory, and now she further prophesied that a woman would ultimately defeat Sisera. Because of Deborah's reputation for wisdom, courage, and reliability, having her accompany Barak's army would be reassuring to the soldiers heading into battle. Sure enough, the Israelites defeated the great army of Jabin, but Sisera managed to slip away and escape.

Enter heroine number three. As Sisera fled the battle-field, he came upon a tent that belonged to a Kenite woman named Jael. Rather than quietly sneaking out the back to safety, Jael formulated a plan to kill the general. She invited Sisera into her tent, and when he asked for water, she gave him milk instead. She also gave him a nice soft blanket and waited until he drifted off to sleep. Then Jael summoned her courage, and with hammer in hand she drove a tent peg into Sisera's temple. When Barak arrived shortly thereafter, the general was already dead at the hands of one brave, heroic woman—just as Deborah had foretold. Clearly, these heroines of old were a force to be reckoned with.[3]

Guys, the women in our lives today, like the women of ancient days, are much stronger and more capable of heroic deeds than we often imagine or acknowledge. Women want and deserve respect. They want a true partnership in marriage, and they are not willing to be a doormat to a dictator, nor should they be.

Women are not looking to be "rescued," as if they were helpless without a man. But in much the same way that a woman can draw out the heroic heart of a man, what we in turn can help them rescue is their sense of innate, God-given beauty, strength, and purpose, which has been under attack in our society. Women are strong and brave and worthy of a heroic partnership. A strong, godly marriage is one between two people joined in faith, created in the image of God as male and female. Together they are heroes in helping those less fortunate. Heroes together in rearing their children.

In the #MeToo era, women are finding their voices, individually and collectively, and becoming bolder about using them. Today's confident woman is not so much "holding out for a hero" as she is wanting to share the adventure of life with a man in touch with his heroic soul. She isn't paralyzed by life, hoping a fairy tale prince will notice her and kiss her so she can function normally again. She is already alive and well—quite capable and strong, with her own dreams and her own courageous voice. She wants to be part of a great love story where her man brings his fully adult, mature self into the relationship in a way that complements her female heart and strength.

Too many men act like overgrown babies waiting for a woman to rescue *them*. It is your job to grow and mature into a spiritually and emotionally secure man. You have to be willing; you have to do the work. When life gets hard or when those old wounds surface, a hero doesn't run off and comfort himself with work or booze or drugs or porn. The hero does what is necessary to heal the wound and live fully from his masculine heart.

Everyday Heroes

What does it look like to be an everyday hero to your wife? Your number one priority as a husband is to be fully present and available. That means doing what needs to be done to identify your baggage and resolve it. It means learning to live from the fullness of your masculine heart, offering your wife and family your strength, energy, vision, encouragement, and care.

We tend to think of a hero as the guy who rescues people from burning buildings, negotiates high-powered business deals, or makes the game-winning touchdown. Those accomplishments are heroic, without a doubt, but don't fall into the trap of idolizing male stereotypes that only serve to make you feel inferior. Everyday heroes are more likely to exhibit what former NFL coach Tony Dungy has called *quiet strength*.[4] What that looks like will vary based on a man's temperament, aptitudes, and other factors, but the common denominator is that everyday heroes have a settled sense of their place in God's eyes. They know their purpose on earth, they live with a sense of meaning and a spirit of adventure, and they pursue and enjoy healthy relationships. Real men and real heroes are not one-dimensional, predictable drones. Real heroes are real men with lives that are far more complex than the stereotypes offered up by our culture. But whatever his particular characteristics, a hero prioritizes serving his wife.

Here's one thing that Dave and I both learned the hard

way: Don't assume you already know what your wife wants and needs. *Ask* her. A real hero will say to his wife, "What can I do to help you? What do you need most right now?" And then he will step in with kindness and grace and does his best to meet the need. It may mean putting down his phone, coming in from the garage, or delaying his trip to the gym. Heroes do whatever it takes to be fully present and available—that's the sort of unselfish sacrifice that touches a woman's heart. A great husband is also a man who knows how to call out the beauty in his wife in every season of life, letting her know that she will always be the only one for him. And when she forgets, perhaps because of unkind voices from her past, the heroic husband helps her remember who she really is: a daughter of the King.

A secure hero-husband will also support his wife's dreams and let her know that he is proud of her talents and accomplishments. He understands her need for girl time and solitude and self-care, and he encourages her to create or explore activities that bring her joy. He loves seeing her grow and blossom, and he will be in the front row applauding her successes, and on the sidelines comforting her and cheering her on when she is hurt or disappointed. Whether she works inside or outside the home—and let's be honest, most women do *both*—he will divvy up the chores in such a way that she doesn't have to carry more than her share. He will be her number one fan, her safe place to land, and the lover of her soul as well as her physical lover.

I (Steve) am so proud of what my wife, Misty, has done

with her life and the lessons she has learned from participating in the Twelve Step group Al Anon for more than twenty years. Now she helps other women in their recovery and restoration process. She is a group facilitator and also sponsors some women who are fortunate enough to have her one-on-one care and focus. Her group members are astounded by her wisdom, and so am I. She is invaluable as a writing partner, and her insights into Scripture always inspire me.

Courage has never been the sole domain of the masculine soul, as any man can attest who has observed a woman giving birth, fighting for her kids, or asserting her right to be heard in a marriage or at work or in the world at large. Women have always had courage and strength in spades; it just comes wrapped in a feminine package.

Though it may be hard for some men to admit, we need women—loving and self-assured women—in order to be our best selves. This isn't something new to our day and age. It has always been true, especially among men who are wise enough to value their wife's intellectual and intuitive gifts. In healthy, long-term marriages, husbands and wives take turns being the other's hero, depending on the day and the circumstances.

John Adams, second president of the United States, had one of our country's most inspiring marriages, a true partnership of intellectual equals. John was brilliant and argumentative, and sometimes he let his ego and temper get the best of him. Abigail was an astute observer of the tumultuous political scene, and thus an invaluable asset to her husband at the birth of our nation. She was his biggest fan, but she was unafraid to confront him when she felt his impulsiveness was out of line. In an era when women were excluded from politics, Abigail Adams was not afraid to speak her mind. And John held her opinion in high esteem. Their mutual respect and deep passion and love for each other, revealed in their many letters to one another—more than 1,100 over the course of their courtship and marriage—are an inspiration.

During Adams's involvement in forming the eventual Constitution of the United States, Abigail wrote to him in March 1776:

> Remember the Ladies, and be more generous and favorable to them than your ancestors. Do not put such unlimited power into the hands of the Husbands. Remember all Men would be tyrants if they could. If particular care and attention is not paid to the Ladies we are determined to foment a Rebellion, and will not hold ourselves bound by any Laws in which we have no voice, or Representation.[5]

No shy, retiring violet here. John Adams referred to Abigail teasingly as being "so saucy!"[6] But this marriage of two brilliant and strong-willed patriots was woven together by an ardent and enduring love. Twenty years after their first meeting, during one of John's many long absences (this time he was in the Netherlands seeking to borrow money for the new American country), Abigail wrote,

> I look back to the early days of our acquaintance
> . . . as to the days of Love and Innocence; and with
> an indescribable pleasure I have seen near a score
> of years roll over our Heads, with an affection
> heightened and improved by time—nor have the
> dreary years of absence in the smallest degree effaced
> from my mind the Image of the dear untitled man to
> whom I gave my Heart.[7]

Many of us guys, left to our own devices, could easily become brooding, self-focused, wounded beasts. The love of a brave, honest, and caring beauty helps us confront our demons and bring out our better angels, both of which help us get in touch with the soul of the hero buried underneath all the false bravado. Being the hero to your wife's heart is a lifelong pursuit, with challenges to overcome and skills to learn in every season of marriage. Ask a husband who has been happily married for fifty or sixty years whether he has learned all he needs to know about loving his wife. If he is honest, he will tell you he is still learning about her, discovering her mind and loving her body as she grows and changes and matures. A man never conquers understanding his woman. He could never settle in for the long haul as if his wife were a book he's finished reading and put on the shelf. She is always evolving and growing, as are you, and that means your marriage is living and changing, with new chapters unfolding, new plot twists and turns, for as long as you both shall live.

Real men understand these truths and value and honor the women in their lives as equal partners.

Your Wife, Your Priority

Most guys arrive at their wedding day with more hormones than wisdom. We all have so much to learn about the art of being a good husband. But as you learn how to love your wife in a way that cares for her unique heart, she will help you become the man God called you to be. This is what makes marriage both a challenge and a joy.

I (Dave) have to admit that I came to marriage with lots of "assembly required" to become a good husband. In fact, my wife and I call the first ten years of our marriage The Great Tribulation because things were so bad. Not long after our wedding, I started working in a parachurch youth ministry. As part of our training, the leadership team told us, "Men, you are now married to the ministry."

What can I say? I was young and vulnerable to persuasive mentors with powerful voices. After all, I had "conquered" marriage (simply by saying "I do"), and now it was time to conquer the world for the sake of God's Kingdom. I not only bought into this dangerous idea but was also naive enough to come home and let Jan know that I was now "married to the ministry." Her reaction was a cool, "I thought you were married to me." The conversation ended quickly. She was not impressed with my spiritual gianthood.

As I took the leaders' admonition to heart and *my* ministry became my top priority, you can imagine the effect it had on our marriage. About ten years in, when I accepted a position in a church as a youth pastor and continued to operate on the principle that ministry was my top priority, my wife became more and more detached from me emotionally, protecting her heart from the pain of abandonment.

But then I met an astute and compassionate man who got me straightened out.

Once a week, a number of pastors and youth leaders would gather at one of the local churches that had a gym to play basketball and have lunch together. It didn't take long for Ron Ritchie, one of the more experienced pastors, to suggest that he and I meet up to eat lunch in his office. I didn't know it at the time, but later I realized I was being mentored by a truly wise man whose life and demeanor I had come to deeply respect. Ron suggested I consider a new way of thinking, a new idea about ministry. First of all, perhaps "my ministry" belonged to God and was a shared ministry with my wife. Then one day he said, "Until your wife is your top priority, neither ministry nor anything else in your life will go right."

Having lived under the old principle of ministry first, family second, I initially pushed back against Ron's advice. But I could not deny the fruit of love, honesty, and joy in his life. His marriage reflected the priority and care he gave to his wife and kids. I wanted that. But it meant letting go of my pride and a decade's worth of accumulated false beliefs. I had to come as a child and open my mind and heart to a wiser and higher truth. In Sermon on the Mount language, I heard God's voice saying, "Dave, you have heard it said that your ministry must be your priority; but I say unto you, make your wife your priority, and ministry will follow naturally." Gradually, through my study of Scripture and through logic and reason, I began to see the error of my former way of thinking. Thankfully, my mentor never gave up on me.

I muted the voices of pride and misguided "spiritual knowledge" and became more humble. I apologized to my wife. I continued listening to wisdom from a seasoned pastor, changed my mind and heart, and altered the entire direction of our lives. The Great Tribulation ended, and we rebooted our marriage on much healthier ground. Since then, God's ministry, not mine, has flowed naturally from the blessing of an honest and real relationship with God and a loving marriage—my true top priorities. It took far too long, but I learned that when marriage comes before the rest, the rest comes easier.

If there is one thing I want you to know about being a heroic husband, it is this: Prioritize your wife. Keep her first in your heart. Greet her like a queen with a kiss in the morning, hug her when you come home at the end of the day, and let her know you missed her. Bless her and wish her a wonderful night's sleep before you go to bed. If you are to be king of your castle, you need a powerful, confident, and well-loved queen at your side. If you treat her like the treasure she is and cherish her love, you will always be her hero at home, co-reigning with confidence and grace over the little kingdom that is your family.

The Emotionally Intelligent Husband

I hope you are comfortable enough in your masculinity to check in with your wife often, to ask her opinions, to value her input and advice. Though God no doubt uses your unique masculine skills to lead your family, the Holy Spirit will also use your wife to help guide and protect you and your family in surprising ways. God gave most women an intuitive gift, and they can read a room, a person, and a situation in ways that most men cannot. Your wife brings her own set of superpowers to your marriage. Ignore them at your peril. If you want to be her superhero, treat her as your heroine. Make sure she is an equal partner in all the major decisions that affect your family. Mutual respect pays great dividends.

John Gottman, a preeminent marriage researcher and therapist, discovered that the happiest marriages are those in which the husband values his wife and allows her to influence him. In fact, a man of high emotional intelligence not only shares his opinions but also asks for and appreciates his wife's input. A man who naturally includes his wife and values her influence in decision-making is much more likely to enjoy a happy marriage. Conversely, writes Kyle Benson, a researcher at the Gottman Institute, "the husband who lacks emotional intelligence rejects his partner's influence because he typically fears a loss of power."[8] By verbally strong-arming or ignoring his wife and not seeking or valuing her opinions, a husband may win the battle, but he is well on his way to losing the war. Typically a marriage with a power-grabbing husband will end in divorce or produce an unhappy and stressful relationship.

An emotionally intelligent husband will show interest in his wife's emotions, listen to and validate her point of view, and try to understand her needs and perspective. He will turn *toward* her instead of putting up a wall and turning away when they hit a problem or emotional roadblock. He will choose the way of *we* over *me*—in other words, a partnership instead of a dictatorship. The reward? According to Kyle Benson, "his relationship, sex life, and overall happiness will be far greater than the man who lacks emotional intelligence."[9]

Creative Conflict

The hardest time for a husband to act heroically is when there is conflict in his marriage. It's easy to be the hero to your wife's heart when all is well and you're living in harmony. But what about when you come to a fork in the road and she cannot see the situation from your point of view? Do you say, "My way or the highway," do you give in to her wishes, or do you . . . what?

Here's a little secret we've learned to help husbands

navigate those flashpoints in a healthy, positive way: When you and your wife are in conflict or have different opinions, the key is for each of you to identify your core need. Then look for a suitable compromise, some way in which your core needs overlap to create a win-win solution. "Core Needs to Compromise" helps couples get unstuck in ways that honor the perspectives of both parties.

Think about a disagreement you might have at some point with your wife. Let's say she's been housebound with the kids all week and wants to go out on a date night with you; but you're exhausted from your own work and are really looking forward to some downtime and relaxing.

She may identify her core need as "getting out of the house and having some fun." Your core need may be "relaxing and cocooning." If you are both open and creative and determined to find a workable solution, several win-win compromise scenarios are possible. For example, you could offer to order pizza, watch the kids, and enjoy a family movie while your wife enjoys a girls' night out with some friends. Or maybe you could order takeout and invite another couple whom you both enjoy over for a relaxing evening on the porch or around the firepit. Or perhaps you and your wife could relax for a couple of hours at home, letting the week roll off your shoulders and enjoying a simple dinner, and then go out for a fancy dessert.

Understanding, creativity, compromise, and looking for a win-win are your best strategies when it comes to being a heroic husband who can go the distance in a happy and healthy marriage.

When you hit a wall in a disagreement, don't just react with whatever comes off the top of your head. Instead, take a step back and look at the situation with a detached sense of curiosity. Pause to identify the core need under your professed desires, and ask your wife to do the same. Look for a creative third-way solution that will meet both of your core needs. If nothing comes up right away, sleep on it, pray over it, and ask God to reveal his win-win answer. You'll be amazed at how well this simple method works to turn a problem into a mutually satisfying project you can work on together. There are no dictators in a healthy marriage. Marriage is a partnership of love and respect, equally given and received.

Rockin' It as Your Daughter's Hero

We want to speak for a moment to dads of daughters about valuing the women in your life. You are most likely your daughter's first hero, and how you treat her—and her mother—will affect her self-worth all her life.

When Madeline was born, I (Steve) saw her as a gift from God. Many years earlier, I had destroyed my first child's life through abortion, and now I was given a child saved by courageous birth parents who refused to have an abortion. I hope that I am a hero to Madeline, because we have always had a close father-daughter bond, and it grows stronger through the years.

But I was not her first hero. That honor goes to her birth mother, who preserved her life and brought her into the world.

Her first male hero was her birth father. He wanted Madeline to have a chance at life. And once she was born, he wanted to be certain she was placed with the right family for her. Before he would agree to give her up, he came over to the hotel where my wife and I were staying and met with us for four hours. He was just a kid himself, but he stayed there hour after hour until he was convinced we were the right ones to raise his newborn child. How uncomfortable it must have been for a sixteen-year-old boy to sit for that long with two strangers while making such a momentous decision. But he did it, and that's what a hero dad does. Once he turned Madeline over to me, I had the responsibility and privilege of bonding with her, nurturing her to adulthood, and becoming her dad hero for a lifetime.

Research has shown that when a daughter has a close and caring relationship with her father, she draws value from it all her life.[10] Sharing athletics or work life or building memories while on vacation are just some of the ways that a dad can be a hero to his daughter, with benefits that are surprisingly far-reaching.

Here are a few ways that being an encouraging and involved dad can help your daughter develop into a happy, balanced, and successful woman:

1. Daughters who have actively engaged fathers who encourage them in academics or athletics are more likely to graduate from college and enter the type of high-paying, demanding jobs that are traditionally

held by men.[11] Interestingly, girls without any brothers are overly represented among the world's political leaders. Why? Without sons, their fathers tended to encourage their daughters to become high achievers. That male mentoring energy wasn't siphoned off to a brother.[12]

You may want to ask yourself whether you are investing a sense of power and can-do spirit into your daughter. If you have sons, it is easy to treat your daughters with a bit more distance, to neglect teaching them skills that would give them a big boost of confidence in the world of men. You can be their hero by showing them how to feel at ease in a man's world. Teach your daughter the skills to hold her own on a baseball field or in a boardroom, even if you also have sons to guide and teach. A woman today is three times more likely to choose the same career path as her dad.[13] This is due in part to changing gender roles, but it also reflects the greater role that fathers play in their kids' lives, as they tend to be much more naturally mentoring than fathers from earlier generations. Helping your daughter develop self-confidence and feel at ease among boys and men will be a fabulous asset for her future.

2. How much does a father influence his daughter's future romantic life? Quite a lot, as it turns out. Research shows that well-fathered daughters are more likely to

have emotionally fulfilling and intimate relationships with men. They are much less likely to be talked into sex and will generally make wiser choices about the type of man they date. They also have more satisfying, long-lasting marriages in general. Surprisingly, dads tend to have more impact on their daughters' future relationships with men than their moms do.[14]

3. Daughters whose dads are heroic (meaning they show up and encourage and love their daughters) are less likely to become depressed or have eating disorders and are more likely to have a healthier body image. Women who had a good dad in their life show physiological markers that indicate they handle stress better. They don't describe men using stressful or negative terms as often.[15]

So, dads, your fathering has long-lasting and far-reaching influence on your daughters. I saw a post on a social media site recently from a woman who was on an airplane that had just landed and was taxiing to the gate. She said that just before they landed the flight attendant announced there was a father at the back of the plane who was worried about making it on time to take his twin daughters to a daddy-daughter dance. When the plane reached the gate, everyone remained seated so the dad could get off first. The passengers even applauded as he sprinted to the exit door. You may not have seen his cape, but that dad was about to be Superman to two very blessed little girls. If you have a daughter, be that kind of hero to her.

Respect for All Women

Unless you've lived in a cave for the past few years, you've probably noticed the emergence of the #MeToo and the #ChurchToo movements that have shifted our society out of its complacency in the way it has too often treated women. For far too long, many men have treated women as objects to be preyed upon, as servants to be used for their pleasure, or as a gender to be put in their place, belittled, or ignored—all to make these insecure men feel temporarily powerful. As Peggy Noonan aptly observed in her weekly *Wall Street Journal* column on December 3, 2017, "At the heart of the current scandals is a simple disrespect and disregard for women."[16] The core issue at the bottom of all verbal and physical abuse, all sexual harassment and misconduct, is a failure on the part of men to value women as our equals, worthy of our respect, regard, and honor. Regrettably, this has been as true in the church as it has been in the world at large.

Women are now saying, enough is enough. Thankfully, real men—men who are in touch with their genuine masculinity, men who know their own value and worth to God, men who believe that women are equal in their value and worth to God—are speaking out in solidarity and agreement.

One of the brave female Christian voices speaking truth to religious power on behalf of multitudes of abused women is Beth Moore, a beloved Bible teacher to millions through her books, videos, and special events. She experienced sexual abuse as a child from someone in her own home. (She has not been more specific than that in her public writing or speaking.) But when, as a little girl, she told her mother what was happening, her mother's response was, "We protect the family."[17]

Church became for her a safe harbor from her unsafe home. Still, she expressed that as a child she'd had a longing to feel safe enough to talk to someone at church about the harm she experienced at home. "I have often wondered what a difference it would have made if that same harbor had not only been a place to hide, but a place to heal. . . . What if I had heard my pastor or my teachers express what I was going through? Call it what it was? Tell me that I wasn't to blame and not be ashamed? . . . What if I had known I wasn't alone? What if I had known that there was help?"[18]

As a result of her ministry, Beth has experienced verbal assaults and misogyny from men in religious leadership. She has also received unwelcome advances from men in ministry, men she once respected. These experiences not only hurt women but also the entire body of Christ.

Sadly, Beth Moore is not alone. Kay Warren, of Saddleback Church in Southern California, recently shared that she also was abused as a little girl, and that the abuse occurred in the church itself. One in four women report they have been sexually harassed or abused. How many never report it? The numbers are likely far, far higher.

There is a term called *sanctuary trauma*, which refers to a second wounding or a second trauma that happens when a person reports the harm they have experienced to someone who should function as a sanctuary of safety, reassurance, and healing, but who instead disbelieves, shuts down, or shuns the victim. This happened in Beth Moore's case, as it also happens in many others. True men, real heroes, provide a safe harbor and safe sanctuary for all women and girls. They do not re-wound them by further abuse, shut them down, belittle or shame them, or dismiss their voices.

One of the male Christian leaders who has been openly supportive of women who have experienced sexual trauma or abuse is pastor and bestselling author Max Lucado. I (Steve) love to have Max on *New Life Live!* because he genuinely cares for people and is a great communicator. He and I have done some speaking together and have appeared together on television. When I took a group of New Life supporters to Bandon Dunes on a golf outing, Max joined us and was such a delight for the men to be with. But during our times together, he never shared about his own abuse. He only recently shared for the first time in public that he was also sexually abused as a young boy by a community leader. So perhaps Max is more prone to believe women and to empathize with their pain.

Max is now calling men to be true heroes to the women in their lives, and to start by asking questions and listening to answers with kindness and understanding. At the GC2 Summit on Responding to Sexual Harassment, Abuse, and

Violence, held at Wheaton College in December 2018, Max told the audience,

> Now is the time for across-the-coffee-table conversations that begin with the words, "Help me to understand what it's like to be a female in this day and age. . . . Help me to understand what it's like to never go on a jog without carrying a canister of mace. . . . Help me to understand what it's like to always be outnumbered in the boardroom. Help me understand what it's like to be hugged chest to chest, unable to break free. Help me to understand what it's like to fear filing a workplace complaint because my supervisors are all male. . . . Help me to understand."[19]

So how do real, heroic men respond in this era of #MeToo?

Real men and real heroes get help before pornography or lust or infidelity become a problem. They stop objectifying women and start seeing them as complete and whole persons, not just a collection of body parts. And as Max Lucado suggests, real men and real heroes talk less, assume less, ask more questions, listen, and seek to understand. They stand up on behalf of women in male circles and talk honestly to other men who are stuck in the Mad Men era—challenging them and bringing them up to speed. If you're on the older end of the spectrum, teach the younger men what you have learned about loving and respecting women and what that should look like in today's dating scene.

What causes a man to take advantage of women? To use them as objects to give him a sexual thrill? To talk down to them or leave them out of leadership in the home and the inner circles of leadership in business and at church? To belittle them in subtle or overt ways?

We believe these things happen when men haven't absorbed the hero's lessons we've written about in these chapters. They don't yet know their value to God, how deeply loved and accepted they are. So they look for love's substitutes in all the wrong places and all the wrong ways. Maybe they didn't have good fathering or good mentoring from men who know how to treat women with the respect and honor they deserve. Since they never saw good role models of men treating women respectfully in their family, they copied the negative patterns they observed instead. (Research shows that men who are abusive or belittling to women usually had fathers who did not treat women with respect and honor.)[20]

A man who doesn't treat women well most likely doesn't have a supportive band of brothers who hold him accountable to a higher calling. The books and ministries that grew out of *Every Man's Battle*, a book I (Steve) wrote with Fred Stoeker and first published in 2000, have shown amazing results using the Band of Brothers concept to hold men accountable to moral purity. Alumni of *Every Man's Battle* are known as Brothers in the Battle. They come to weekend intensives to encourage other men who are getting help for the first time, and also to review and revive helpful truths that work to keep them free. Brothers in the Battle is a powerful group that, alongside a program called Sustained Victory, helps men stay pure and free. Most men need a place to be honest about pornographic temptations—which are so prevalent online and in all forms of media—and learn how to deal with them in a way that is honoring to God, to themselves, and to women.

Men often fall into temptation by playing dangerous games of flirtation or sexual innuendo with women (even in ministry organizations) in search of a hit of adrenaline, because they feel they have lost their mojo, their mission, or their higher calling and passion in other areas of their lives. They may have stopped putting effort into keeping their own marriage alive and passionate. They're always on the hunt for the next "prize" rather than focused on the adventure of cherishing their own wife and rising to the challenge of nourishing her love for a lifetime.

Where can men find a biblical role model for how to treat women? They needn't look any further than to the Son of God himself. Jesus elevated women when other men put them down. He protected the life and dignity of the woman caught in adultery by telling her accusers that the one who hadn't sinned should throw the first stone. Interestingly, the men let the stones drop from their hands and walked away, from the oldest to the youngest.[21] Perhaps the older men left first because they had experienced more years of falling into sin and were more acquainted with their own failures.

When the disciples chided the woman with the alabaster jar for coming to see Jesus and pouring expensive perfume on his head, Jesus rebuked them. When the men—applying their male logic to the situation—complained that the perfume could have been sold and the money given to the poor, Jesus stopped them in their tracks. "Why are you bothering this woman? She has done a beautiful thing to me."[22] Then he added that her act of love would be told, and long remembered, wherever the gospel was shared throughout the world.[23]

Jesus spoke to and treated women as equals and as friends, often defying society's norms by bantering with one of them by a well, chatting with them in their homes, comforting them in their grief, and answering their deep spiritual questions. It was women who never left his side when he was dying on the cross, his mother who did not turn away in his moment of greatest agony. It was women who prepared his body for burial, and it was a woman who first saw him after his resurrection.[24]

Remember what we said earlier about the courage and bravery of women? They are courageous in ways that sometimes escape us men when the really hard times hit. They are often more compassionate by nature, more expressive in their love, and more able to endure heartache, and they often think clearly about how to be there for the long haul to help someone who is in pain. Women embody the female attributes of God—his tender, nurturing, patient, loving, intuitive, and intimate side. When we mistreat or take advantage of a woman, we are diminishing someone who represents so many aspects of God—aspects that we guys need in our lives in order to become balanced and whole. It sounds contradictory, but to be the whole masculine hero you want to be, you must respect, accept, love, and allow yourself to be influenced by the good and wise women God places in your life.

By Way of Balance

As with all movements, we can overcorrect as a society. Sometimes in our efforts to "level the playing field" we only make things uneven or unfair in the opposite direction. It's important to realize that encouraging women to rise to their rightful and natural place as coequals in our society doesn't mean we have to put down our innate masculine qualities and strengths. Male and female are designed to be complementary—to complete one another and bring wholeness. There's a popular saying in the women's movement that "a woman needs a man like a fish needs a bicycle," but that isn't true.[25] We need *each other*. We were made for each other. What is needed is for men to treat women with the honor and respect they deserve for simply being who they are. Then women will be free to respond in kind.

Women *and* men are right to expect to be treated fairly, kindly, and respectfully. Boys *and* girls need to know they are equally valued and loved. We need marriages in which both genders are equally celebrated, where children grow up seeing their parents love and respect each other in normal, everyday ways.

This often happens most naturally as husbands and wives work together as a team, for a shared goal, living with each other in ways that are mutually encouraging. So much about valuing each other will be caught rather than taught. Even something as simple as putting together a piece of furniture, working together in the kitchen, or tackling a home-improvement project together can be a lesson to children about how men and women cooperate and value each other's help. Or let your kids see you and your wife playing a game—competing good-naturedly while also complimenting and encouraging each other.

Play nice and play fair. Compete with good sportsmanship. Encourage and support one another. Cooperate on mutual goals and projects. Little eyes are watching you both, and your kids will learn to emulate in their future relationships how you and your wife treat each other now. So be sure to model what you want them to learn. Treat your wife as you want your son to treat *his* wife someday. Treat your wife the way you want a young man to treat your daughter someday.

We have friends in their sixties, a happily married couple, who love to snuggle on the couch together in the evening while watching whodunit-type mysteries, especially the British shows. They each try to guess who the murderer might be, searching for and sharing the clues they observe as the plot unfolds.

"When one of us figures out who the culprit is, or solves a

clue correctly," the husband told us, "the other will acknowledge it by saying something like, 'Brilliant observation!'—
with a heavy English accent of course."

"It's a small thing," the wife said, "but we have so much
fun. We compliment each other on figuring out clues, taking
turns feeling like an ace detective. We've become a sort of
couch-based detective team, cheering each other on, like
Sherlock and Watson."

This is a great example of what John Gottman calls the
"we-ness" in a healthy marriage versus a you-against-me men-
tality that erodes love.[26] Look for small opportunities to work
as a team, to be a couple who solves life's mysteries together.

If You See Something, Say Something

If you want to be a hero to your woman's heart, you must
recognize her value and cherish the wisdom, strength, beauty,
and gentle compassion she brings to your life—and don't
forget to give her the honor she is due.

"I admire my wife so much," one guy told us, "and I
brag on her amazing abilities to others. But I often forget to
verbalize these thoughts to *her*. It's like if I *think* it, I believe
she must *know* it, by osmosis or something."

A good rule of thumb is that when you notice something
admirable in your wife—how she works hard both on the
job and at home, how she loves and plays with your kids or
grandkids, her creativity or her spunk as she tackles a project,
the way her eyes twinkle when she ponders a new idea—open

your mouth and tell her. Leave nothing unsaid. In sports lingo, "Don't hold anything in the tank; leave it all on the field."

Life is a onetime shot. Put your heart out there, and let your woman know how much you love and admire her. Notice the little things and tell her about them. Treat her with respect and honor and praise. That's what real hero-husbands do.

A wife of noble character who can find? She is
worth far more than rubies. Her husband has
full confidence in her . . . and he praises her. . . .
Honor her for all that her hands have done.[27]

7

MASTERING YOUR MIND

Heroic Secret #7: Win the War Within

*We faced conflict from every direction,
with battles on the outside and fear on the inside.*

2 CORINTHIANS 7:5

"**L**ife is difficult."

"Life is good, just as it is."

Live long enough, and you'll know that both these quotes are simply and profoundly true.

The first quote is the opening line from one of the most famous self-help books of the last century: M. Scott Peck's *The Road Less Traveled,* published in 1978.

The second quote is from a memoir written by George Dawson, a 103-year-old slave's grandson who learned to read at the age of ninety-eight.

Perhaps you are curious about what else these two men had to say. Here are two extended quotes:

> Life is difficult.
>
> This is a great truth, one of the greatest truths. It is a great truth because once we truly see this truth, we transcend it. Once we truly know that life is difficult—once we truly understand and accept it—then life is no longer difficult. Because once it is accepted, the fact that life is difficult no longer matters.[1]
>
> **M. SCOTT PECK**

> Life ain't going to be perfect, but things will work out. People come to visit and I always tell them not to worry. If you got something to eat, don't worry, be grateful. . . .
>
> Things will be all right. People need to hear that.

Life is good, just as it is. There isn't anything I would change about my life. . . .

Be happy for what you have. Help somebody else instead of worrying.[2]

GEORGE DAWSON

Life is difficult. It is not fair. Expecting it to be otherwise makes it more difficult. Expect life to be hard; accept that it comes with complexities and challenges, pain and sorrow, and dozens of daily hassles, and it won't be nearly so difficult.

Life is good, just as it is. It isn't perfect, but if you choose gratitude, you'll see goodness everywhere.

We can hold both truths at the same time: Life is difficult. Life is good.

Two Tracks at the Same Time

Most often, life is not as much like a roller coaster—with ups and downs and twists and turns—as it is like two trains on parallel tracks going at the same time: one full of joy and blessings, the other full of difficulties, challenges, and pain.

If we were to ask you, "What's going wrong in your life right now? What's worrying you? What sometimes keeps you up at night? What is difficult?"—and then, "What's good, what is going right? What are you grateful for? What are your greatest blessings?"—most of you could share examples of both without thinking very hard. Both elements of your life would easily bubble to the surface.

Life is rarely all sunshine or all rain. Though most of us have enjoyed some blessed times of refreshment when life is incredibly good and all is well, we have also experienced seasons of suffering when it seems we're facing one crisis after another. Often it's not just one thing; it's two or three.

If you have had one or more of these seasons, you can probably recall the year or years that you survived. Maybe you've even named them:

The Great Depression of 1985.

The Marriage Crisis of 2005.

My Teenager's Prodigal Years, 1998–2001.

Sometimes life sends a lightning bolt into our lives and leaves us reeling from sudden and dramatic bad news or a bad experience. As we were writing this chapter, a tornado ripped through downtown Nashville in the wee hours of the morning—one of fifteen tornadoes to touch down in Tennessee over a two-day period. Nobody anticipated it. There was no time to prepare. Waking up to destruction all around, hearing of good people suddenly gone with the wind—literally—is disorienting and traumatic. Some sorrows in life come with a heavy dose of shock attached to them.

Not long after the Tennessee tornadoes, the United States found itself in the throes of the global coronavirus pandemic. Perhaps by the time this book reaches you, life will have returned to some semblance of normal. But as of today, experts are estimating that this situation, which has upended our country in profound ways—medically, socially, and economically—may last for many more months, perhaps even eighteen or more.

At first, the crisis felt sudden and anxiety was high, but as the months wore on, it began to feel chronic, and the novelty had definitely worn off.

Whether it is a sudden shocking event—a lightning bolt that upsets the calm in our lives—or it's something that feels more like a dark cloud hanging over our heads or a drizzling rain in the background of our lives that never seems to go away, none of us will get out of this life without facing challenges and conflicts, sorrows and disappointments, hassles and heartache, and even agony and grief. But that doesn't mean we have to like it.

Part of the reason that guys love heroic stories and movies is that there is something within us that wants to right a wrong, fix a hurt, stop a bad guy, and save the world. One of the greatest feelings a man can experience happens when he can stop a bad situation, rescue someone from danger, or fix something that's broken. Guys live for those moments when they can be the hero and help in a crisis. Cue the soundtrack from *Rocky*. Put on your Superman cape.

The hardest thing for a man to deal with is a situation he can't easily fix or control: Cancer. A tragic accident. A long-term illness. A loved one who chooses to walk away. Someone else's addiction. His adult child's risky choices. Mental illness in someone he loves. A parent with dementia. Being laid off. A business that goes under. A global pandemic.

What is the worst feeling in the world for a man? Feeling helpless to change a painful situation.

Men cope with crises and challenges in unique ways, ways that tend to be very different from the methods that women use to handle stress and pain. Women tend to reach out, to "tend and mend." A man's way of coping doesn't often involve calling a friend to meet up and chat over coffee or taking a casserole to a buddy who is sick.

Not at all. We men have our own strategies.

How Men Cope When Life Gets Hard

From our years of observing and being members of the male species, we have noticed that men tend to handle life's various upsets in five common ways. They either try to *fix* them, *endure* them, *withdraw* from or *avoid* them, *escape* them through addiction, or just *get mad*. Some of these coping skills are good, some are bad, and some are a mixture of both.

After we take a look at these five typical responses, we will share what we believe is a more heroic way of handling hardships. However, like all the lessons in this book, it will take training and practice for this "better way" to become a natural skill.

Fix Them

Men usually excel at handling problems and crises that we can control or fix in a reasonable amount of time. Undoubtedly you've heard that *when the going gets tough, the tough get going.*

Men love this adage. It has that testosterone-loaded, can-do energy that he-men go for. For short-term issues with clear problems and solutions, this is a guy's preferred response: *Find a solution and make it work.*

Git-r-done!

LARRY THE CABLE GUY

Guys actually get an emotional kick, a shot of pleasure, out of solving a problem or fixing a clear-cut issue. Why? Fixing things appeals to the natural hero within us. Few things excite men more than encountering a challenge they can solve with their wits, brawn, or raw talent. Whether a bank statement won't balance correctly, a faucet is leaky, someone is stranded on the side of the road, or someone is gasping for breath amid a medical emergency, men are wired to help. When we're successful and people are grateful, we get a shot of happy endorphins. Or as we like to call it, the "hero's high." We believe this is God-created brain wiring, one of the ways that we are inspired to help each other every day.

If we can help solve a problem, that's awesome. The challenge, however, comes when a problem or heartache isn't readily fixable. Men tend to hate these kinds of issues. We loathe the helpless feeling of not being able to control and fix incoming trouble.

Endure

Endurance is another coping skill that men use when life gets difficult. Most men understand how to endure; and to a reasonable extent, this is a skill that comes in handy. Endurance is a necessary, if unpleasant, emotional bridge to get us from here to there, from bad to better. Endurance takes its own kind of courage. Endurance is putting one foot in front of the other; it is hanging on and hanging in there. It doesn't offer the immediate joy of fixing a problem, but it has its own reward—fortitude. Staying power. The process of staying alive until life feels worth living again.

Heroism . . . is endurance for one moment more.

GEORGE F. KENNAN

Endurance may not look heroic, but it often is. It can look like a friend of ours, recently widowed, who is disoriented and grieving the loss of his beloved wife of many decades. He shared with us his experience of the first morning he woke up without her. He forced himself to brew a single cup of coffee, forgoing for the first time in decades pouring coffee into the second mug he used to take to his sweetheart with a good-morning kiss. He'd never realized how hard it could be to just get out of bed and make himself a cup of coffee. Brave hearts sometimes must endure their way into hope and joy and meaning again, especially after tremendous loss.

Sometimes you just have to keep living until you feel alive again. You hang on until help arrives or the grief subsides.

Endurance is what gets us through everything from remodeling a kitchen to undergoing radiation treatments to surviving a war to getting through the awfulness of grief.

The writer of Hebrews tells us that Jesus "endured the cross" while "despising the shame." How did he endure? He kept his eyes fixed on "the joy that was set before him."[3] If you've ever been in the delivery room during labor, you may know that one technique for helping the expectant mother to stay calm is to have a focal point to look at when she is having a contraction. This can be anything from a photo of a baby to a beautiful scene in nature to a piece of art she loves. As she labors through the ultimate endurance contest, she draws strength from the image of the joy set before her—the cessation of pain, the fruit of her labor, a newborn child.

In a similar way, men need a focal point, a "joyful image" to help them endure the worst of times. The late Senator John McCain endured incredible pain, regular beatings, and ongoing torture while he was a prisoner of war in Vietnam. "'Three things kept me going,' he said. 'Faith in God, faith in my fellow prisoners and faith in my country.'"[4] These were his focal points when life was harder than we can adequately comprehend.

To endure, heroes must have a clear vision of what lies on the other side of the current suffering and pain, and they must hold on to that image like an emotional life preserver, remembering that "our light and momentary troubles"[5] will someday give way to heaven's glory, and all the pain will seem like merely a blip in time.

In *The Return of the King*, J. R. R. Tolkien wrote of the weariness and dread that Frodo and Sam, two fellow travelers and heroes in the making, felt on a particularly long and dangerous journey. They knew the future held uncertainty and likely dark times. As they were resting at night, Sam looked up at the sky:

> There, peeping among the cloud-wrack above a dark tor high up in the mountains, Sam saw a white star twinkle for a while. The beauty of it smote his heart, as he looked up out of the forsaken land, and hope returned to him. For like a shaft, clear and cold, the thought pierced him that in the end the Shadow was only a small and passing thing: there was light and high beauty for ever beyond its reach.[6]

Unhealthy endurance is a refusal to enter the battle, a fear of risk. It is really *avoidance* with a false label. Healthy endurance is about staying engaged with life and with other people, persisting on the journey and holding fast to the good path with the end game of glory in sight.

Withdraw or Avoid

If a painful circumstance rages or plods on too long, or the artillery is coming from all sides and nothing is helping, or nothing he does changes anything—a man can feel an overwhelming loss of control over his life. This is the danger zone. Sometimes men withdraw, like an animal into the forest, too beleaguered to communicate what they are feeling. They get quiet. They play video games or watch TV. They may get easily agitated. They go silent and get lost in the wilderness of their own thoughts. Their wives and kids feel helpless and lonely, trying again and again to draw them out or catch their attention, only to fail.

You cannot find peace by avoiding life.

MICHAEL CUNNINGHAM, *THE HOURS*

There is such a thing as healthy withdrawal—times when we purposefully unplug from the intensity of life to recharge our batteries. It's healthy to take time off occasionally, to rest, to do nothing for a while to restore your energy and your soul—an extended Sabbath, if you will. Luke's Gospel says that Jesus "would often slip away to the wilderness and pray" after ministering to crowds of hurting people.[7]

Healthy withdrawal has a purpose. It has a starting point and an ending point. And we don't just disappear from the radar—we let our loved ones know what's up. We use the time to rest our bodies and restore our souls, and then we reenter daily life—with all its complexities and problems—with renewed focus and energy.

Unhealthy withdrawal doesn't have a designated end

point. It doesn't inform others of what is happening inside. It dodges offers of help and goes to lonely places without any purpose other than to avoid or hide from the problem.

Escape through Addiction

When life gets hard, some men turn to mind-altering substances or activities—something to give them an artificial buzz or a high to mask the painful reality they face but can't control or change. This can lead to substance abuse and the addiction cycle. Some guys use porn like a drug, a brief diversion from reality and pain. Some guys can also become adrenaline junkies—seeking the thrill that comes with dangerous activities, extreme sports, gambling, or daredevil stunts. They go looking for a rush that will temporarily numb their fear, worry, or despair. When life feels out of control, addiction gives a man an artificial sense of power.

Once an addiction takes hold, it can quickly turn from temporarily lessening the pain of life to becoming a master over every waking moment, eventually adding exponentially to our pain. We can find ourselves enslaved to an insatiable inner monster that demands to be fed even as it numbs us to all the normal pleasures of life. It can eventually change our personality and sear a healthy conscience. And as singer James Taylor pointed out, it can rob us of years of the normal maturing and growth that comes from facing, grappling with, and healing from painful and trying circumstances.

Times of crisis are not something to escape from or avoid.

They are an invitation to get in touch with your inner hero, the part of you that discovers, through experience, that you can do all things through Christ who strengthens you.[8] Crisis and pain test our mettle. Often what we think is happening *to* us (to hurt us) is actually happening *for* us (to grow us up).

One thing that addiction does is, it freezes you. You don't develop, you don't learn the skills by trial and error of having experiences and learning from them, and finding out what it is you want, and how to go about getting it, by relating with other people. You short-circuit all of that stuff and just go for the button that says this feels good over and over again. So you can wake up, as I did, at the age of 36, feeling like you're still 17.

JAMES TAYLOR

We have both spent years helping people recover from all kinds of addictions. It is a deep calling, and we feel enormous compassion for those who have fallen into the trap of addiction and gotten caught in its grasp. Though harmful activities or substances can give you the illusion that you're a superhero, you will always wake up at the end of the addiction cycle feeling weak, defeated, and stuck.

Getting high or numbing out may feel good temporarily, but it is in no way a healthy response to life's pain or challenges. When the drug wears off, when the compulsive behavior is over, the pain and challenges will still be there, and your addiction will only add to the pile of problems you face.

Learn to just say no. And if it's too late, if you are already stuck in an addiction, get help. Join a Twelve Step program. Go to an AA or NA meeting or a Life Recovery meeting. See your doctor or addiction therapist and get into a treatment program. Sometimes you need to be a hero to yourself first by asking for help from people who have been there, people who have conquered the monster of addiction and know how to point the way to freedom.

Addiction can sneak up on any man, given the right circumstances in a low moment. Become the hero of your own soul, and choose life over addiction by asking for help.

Get Mad

Many men, when they can't fix a situation, a relationship, or a problem, turn to the intensity of anger, even violence, to dispel their feelings of helplessness.

Did you know that anger is almost always a secondary emotion? Underneath the anger there is usually fear and a sense that there is something you can't control. For some guys, frustration or anxiety becomes their emotional baseline, and it takes very little to set them off into fits of anger. They kick the dog, yell at their wife or kids, or pop off at their boss. Anytime a man feels helpless to alter what is happening in his life, anger can be a common, almost habitual, response. Some men become addicted to the emotional release that unchecked anger gives them in the moment.

Unchecked anger sends a jolt of adrenaline to the neural

system—and for a moment it blocks out every other emotion: fear, worry, insecurity. But it also blocks the brain's normal reasoning and the ability to exercise self-control. Anger often leaves a man feeling guilty, and it can leave behind wreckage in relationships that sometimes cannot be repaired.

People with anger issues are often sent to anger management classes, which can be very beneficial for some people. But if there is damage or dysfunction in the temporal lobes, no amount of class time is going to resolve the issue. When there are issues with the temporal lobes, the underlying biological problem needs to be addressed. . . . Any co-occurring disorders—such as ADHD, anxiety, depression, or addiction—also need to be treated to aid in the healing process.

DR. DANIEL AMEN

Though anger is often a conscious choice, we want to mention something that could prove helpful for men with impulsive anger issues.

Some men are set off very quickly and easily; their personality becomes kidnapped by their emotions, and their anger can turn into a rage that feels truly uncontrollable. Of course, substance abuse can also ramp up anger and override logic, and it is a common factor in male violence. But sometimes, especially in men who played contact sports, the volatility can stem from organic sources or old brain injuries— even seemingly minor concussions from playing sports as a kid or any kind of blow to the head from an accident.

If a guy's anger is knee-jerk or out of control, he may be helped by medication, supplements, or other interventions that will bring more blood flow to the parts of the brain that affect rational thought and calm down overactivity in the temporal lobe.

In *This Is Your Brain on Joy*, Dr. Earl Henslin tells of counseling several couples characterized by husbands who had uncontrollable anger. He paused the marriage therapy sessions and sent the men to get SPECT brain scans and evaluations. All the men were given corrective protocols, and those who followed the protocols saw their marriages improve immensely. Dr. Henslin studied under Dr. Daniel Amen, a world-renowned brain expert and psychiatrist who has written several books about overcoming brain disorders and optimizing brain health, including *Change Your Brain, Change Your Life* and *Feel Better Fast and Make It Last*.

Mastering Your Mind the Hero's Way

One thing we can always control is our thoughts about our circumstances. That pretty much covers every situation. A man who can control his thoughts is able to rule his mind and body.

For those of us who are prone to react to our circumstances, it's important to understand that we always have the power to choose our response. The opportunity may be fleeting and small, but as we become aware of the interlude between stimulus and response, we will find it holds the key to our growth and our freedom.

What if you knew you possessed a superpower that would allow you to get to a place of inner peace almost instantly, no matter what was happening around you?

What if you could be quietly joyful, focused, and engaged with others no matter what difficulties you encountered?

What if you could be grateful no matter what challenges, sorrows, and losses were in your way?

If you could be completely content on the inside regardless of your outward circumstances, wouldn't you feel the greatest kind of freedom imaginable? If you could master your own mind and spirit, with your emotions no longer tied to what happens next, or what happened in the past, or what's happening now, wouldn't you feel like Superman, mentally soaring above the madness into the wild blue yonder of perspective and peace? And what if, from this place of calm and freedom, you were able to make better practical choices in challenging times?

Everything can be taken from a man but one thing: the last of the human freedoms—to choose one's attitude in any given set of circumstances, to choose one's own way. . . . When we are no longer able to change a situation . . . we are challenged to change ourselves.

VIKTOR FRANKL, *MAN'S SEARCH FOR MEANING*

The good news is that this settled state of mind and heart is entirely possible. The bad news is that it goes completely against our nature, because we are creatures of habit. Like Velcro, our brains tend to be "sticky" for negativity while at the same time acting like Teflon toward positive thinking—that is, unless we proactively, consciously work to master our minds. It won't happen overnight, but if you are willing to work at taming your negative thoughts and practicing new, positive ways of seeing the world, you will gradually form new neural pathways in your brain until one day you find that you are simply a calmer, more centered person. Anxiety, worry, fear, and anger will no longer control you.

You can attain an ongoing state of peace and joy, but it will take soul work to transform your mind. When life gets really hard and the battle is raging on every side, you must have the mindset of an Olympian, training yourself in the art of renewing your mind, capturing every thought that doesn't serve you well, and changing your perspective into one that lifts you up and encourages you.

You don't have to do it alone. If you yield to the Holy Spirit, he will constantly speak the truth to you so that in the midst of a difficult battle—perhaps against anxiety, sorrow, or fear—you can keep your head straight by tossing aside the lies that cause unnecessary emotional and spiritual pain.

As I (Dave) have gotten older, I've had to face the reality of aging and some of the limitations and challenges that come with it. One of the most difficult struggles I've had to face, accept, and roll into my new reality is a diagnosis of Parkinson's disease. As Michael J. Fox, a fellow Parkinson's sufferer, has said, "I can't always control my body the way

I want to, and I can't control when I feel good or when I don't. I *can* control how clear my mind is. And I *can* control how willing I am to step up if somebody needs me."[9] This is not an easy path. Like Frodo and Sam on their journey to Mordor, the future for me is uncertain and likely filled with challenges and some dark days. And like Sam, I find I am looking up more and also looking deeper within myself.

I'm gaining a new appreciation for what the apostle Paul discovered as his body aged and he began to regard his physical form as a "jar of clay" that held the true treasure of his spirit and soul—his "inner man." As he wrote to his friends in Corinth, "We do not lose heart. Though our outer self is wasting away, our inner self is being renewed day by day."[10]

But I'm not going to lie; it is a daily practice—soul work—to wake up and get myself "centered down," as the Quakers like to say, and to tackle and tame the thoughts that would drive me to depression and despair and give them to God for alteration, repair, and renewing of my mind. In the following section, I will share with you a method that has been extremely helpful in keeping my mind focused on the good and the best, even though my body often refuses to work well.

If you aren't dealing with tough stuff right now, trust me: The day will come when you are in the middle of a dark woods, feeling as lost as a little kid. When you get to that place, revisit this chapter. You may find it helpful.

Thought by Thought

True heroes learn the secrets of contentment from masters who are skilled in the art of taming their thoughts. The apostle Paul speaks of "the renewing of your mind" and "bringing every thought into captivity to the obedience of Christ."[11] How do you transform your mind? How do you renew it? How do you take on the mind of Christ?

It starts with one little thought.

If you know anything about Twelve Step recovery programs, you've heard the adage, "One day at a time." It's a great way to live.

We have discovered a method to tame and master a runaway or angst-filled mind one *thought* at a time. We base this method, in part, on 2 Corinthians 10:5, where Paul writes, "We demolish arguments and every pretension that sets itself up against the knowledge of God, and we take captive every thought to make it obedient to Christ."[12]

We like Paul's word picture of taking every thought captive—every crazy, careening thought, one at a time—and presenting it to Jesus for remodeling and reshaping. As we bring every thought into obedience to Christ, he transforms our thinking with thoughts that are more encouraging and more true than those that were creating angst, worry, fear, and anger.

We encourage you to try it. We call it "Four Steps to an Inner Miracle."

Step 1: Write down any thought that seems to be troubling you, anything that has kidnapped your attention or is causing you anger or pain. Be honest. Tell it like it is to God. He can take it. If something has been troubling you for a while now, write it down and take a clear look at it.

But what if you have a whole bunch of troubling thoughts going around in your head like rats on a wheel? That's okay. You can get to them, one at a time. Instead of allowing the wheel to spin out of control into "thought overwhelm," just choose the one thought that is causing you the most heartache, anger, or anxiety, and write it on a piece of paper.

Don't try to accomplish this as a mental exercise—write it down. The simple act of writing something on paper accomplishes two important things: It gets the thought out of your head and exposes it to the cold light of day. Sometimes just seeing the words in writing can start to change your perspective.

Step 2: Now that you have written down the one thought that worries you the most, ask yourself, *Is this the truth?* No doubt you've heard the saying, "You will know the truth, and the truth will set you free."[13] Would it surprise you to know that Jesus is the one who said it? But what was the truth he was talking about? If we read the statement in the context of John 8:12-59, we see that the truth to which Jesus was referring is the truth about himself—that he is the Son of God, sent by his Father into the world to accomplish the purpose of setting people free from the power of sin and death.

So as you consider your "one thought" and ask yourself,

Is this the truth? it's important to look at the answer in the context of a larger truth: *Jesus* is the truth, and the truth about Jesus puts everything else in perspective.[14] Consider this: Just moments after Jesus said, "You will know the truth, and the truth will set you free," he also said, "If the Son sets you free, you will be free indeed."[15] Are you starting to see the power (and the wisdom) in taking every thought captive to the obedience of Christ?

Step 3: Having declared the truth about your one thought, how do you hand it over to Jesus? Through prayer—which simply means talking to the Lord. Ask him to give you passages of Scripture, calming thoughts, word pictures, or bits of praise songs or hymns to replace the negative thought you're surrendering to him. As these calming elements come to mind, write them down so you won't forget. I (Steve) will often recite Psalm 23, mentally going to green pastures and quiet waters. I visualize the Good Shepherd taking care of all my needs as I relax and breathe beside him, telling myself, *He's got this; I don't have to worry about a thing.* Sometimes I remind myself of the comforting prayer of Julian of Norwich: "All shall be well; and all manner of thing shall be well."[16] And I imagine myself well and strong and being just fine.

Step 4: After handing your thoughts over to Jesus, think of five things to be grateful for right now. Gratitude blocks fearful thoughts. And it changes our perspective. Gratitude brings us to the here and now and keeps our thoughts from scampering toward the future. Here are my five thoughts today:

1. Today I am well, and my family is well.
2. We have a lovely, warm home.
3. It is springtime. I can take a walk with my family and enjoy the beauty of nature.
4. There is plenty of food in the pantry; we can make a big, healthy meal tonight.
5. I have access to so much great music and can play something uplifting to elevate the mood around here.

After all of this, I've almost forgotten what I was worried about. Instead I'm wondering, *What music should I ask my smart speaker to play? What would be fun to make for dinner? When's a good time to take a family walk?*

When I've taken that one thought and surrendered it to Jesus, he has often given me a half dozen or more happier, better, and just-as-true thoughts to dwell on. I feel more fully present to myself and my family. I'm "Dad, the Hero" again instead of "Dad, the Depressed Dud."

Let's review the Four Steps to an Inner Miracle:

1. Write down the one thought that is nagging at you the most—the thought that is causing you the most concern, worry, or fear.
2. Put your thought to the test by asking, *Is it true?* How does it stack up with the greater truth that Jesus came to set you free from the power of sin and

death? Are you willing and able to accept that Jesus has the power to set you free?

3. Give your thought to Jesus, and ask him to replace it with images, verses, prayers, hymns, poems, or anything else he wants to give you to calm your soul. Meditate on these thoughts and write them down.

4. Write down five things you are grateful for today.

It isn't so much what happens to us that causes pain; it's our *thoughts* about what happens to us that tend to drag us down. God doesn't give us the strength for tomorrow until . . . tomorrow. But he will give us everything we need to handle what's going on right now.

You have turned on my light!
The Lord my God has made my darkness turn to light.
Now in your strength I can scale any wall, attack any troop.

PSALM 18:28-29, TLB

We have found that the Four Steps to an Inner Miracle method helps to tame our runaway thoughts and centers us in the present moment. We encourage you to practice it every time your thoughts begin to spiral, each time you hit an emotional wall, and whenever you face a daunting challenge. We're confident that you will not only feel better almost immediately but also steadily build new neural pathways that will change you into a calmer, more peaceful man in any and all situations. Yours will be the cool head that prevails, no matter what life throws your way.

Whatever happens, you are in Christ, and Christ is victorious.

8

GET READY TO SOAR

Final Thoughts on the Soul of a Hero

For a time it looked as if all the adventures were coming to an end; but that was not to be.

C. S. LEWIS, *THE LION, THE WITCH AND THE WARDROBE*

You may think that your time for adventure, your chance for heroic journeys within and without are long past. But even though you may be at the end of a chapter, you are not at the end of the book of your life. Not unless you are drawing your final breath. Whatever the challenge, you and God have many more stories yet to write and live, and daily opportunities to choose the more heroic path. Just like Christopher Reeve.

As you are no doubt aware, Reeve was the handsome, muscled, charming actor who played Superman in the 1978–1987 versions of the movie. How tragic and ironic it was when he was paralyzed in 1995 after being thrown from a horse. In an instant, his life changed dramatically. It's one thing to play a hero in a movie; it's quite another to play one in real life, when all your dreams lie dashed at your feet. And yet those are the moments when heroes are made. Courage isn't required when everything is easy and good. Bravery implies there is something to fear. Pressing forward anyway and overcoming the challenge is the mark of a hero.

In his post-accident memoir, *Still Me*, Reeve wrote, "A hero is an ordinary individual who finds the strength to persevere and endure in spite of overwhelming obstacles."[1] And that is precisely what Christopher Reeve did for the next nine years of his life. He overcame tremendous obstacles, championed others with disabilities, gave all his love and encouragement to his beloved wife, and left a legacy of kindness and courage for his children—a path for them to follow.

A hero isn't born ready to fly; he is built by the choices he makes. But even if he has made some bad choices or life has dealt him some rough cards, he can overcome that adversity, by God's grace, and show others the way forward. Even the greatest heroes have setbacks, doubts, weaknesses, mix-ups, and U-turns. In fact, these are the very things God uses to strengthen us, to grow our superpowers, and to change us for the better. Tom Hanks, playing an unlikely hero as a baseball coach in the film *A League of Their Own*, said this about playing baseball at the highest levels: "It's supposed to be hard. If it wasn't hard, everyone would do it. The hard [is] what makes it great."[2] As in baseball, so in life. When men look back at the events that shaped and formed them, they realize it is often the hard things they overcame that made their lives great.

With that in mind, let's take one last look at the Soul Hero lessons we've explored.

Lesson 1: Come Empty

Begin as a Child

Here we talked about coming to God empty-handed, with a childlike mind, devoid of pride, ready to learn. It is good to grow and mature, but never leave your childlike heart behind. Stay in touch with the part of you that is open and curious. Trust your Father to be there for you, come what may.

Lesson 2: Your True Identity

You Are Who God Says You Are

Who you truly are, your real identity as a beloved child-son of a Father who is wild about you, is foundational to the soul of a hero. Return again and again to this truth when your own voice or the voices of the world say anything other than this central and eternal truth. You are beloved.

Lesson 3: The Dad Factor

Men Need Mentors

Whether men have father wounds or father blessings or a mixture of both, they need the approval and encouragement of a man who plays a fatherly role in their life. Most men need many good mentors over a lifetime to discover the hero within and grow into who they want to be. Be proactive about seeking and finding and valuing them.

Lesson 4: Sidekicks for the Soul Journey

You're Gonna Need Brothers

Here we explored the need to gather your own band of brothers, friends and peers you can depend on and who can depend on you in all of life's ups and downs, challenges and triumphs. There are no successful Lone Rangers in the hero's journey. You'll need to hustle up a posse.

Lesson 5: Your Mission, Should You Choose to Accept It

Find Your Earthly Purpose

In this chapter we talked about discovering your calling and your unique superpowers. Men need a purpose bigger than themselves, something that makes them want to jump out of bed in the morning and start their day. Take time to uncover your talents and your mission.

Lesson 6: Being a Real Man in #MeToo Times

Love and Respect Her Heart

As Bob Dylan sang, "The times they are a-changin'"—and for the better, in terms of raising the bar for how men should treat women. This chapter explores the balance and blessing of loving your wife, treating her as an equal in your marriage, and respecting and honoring all the gifts she brings to your life.

Lesson 7: Mastering Your Mind

Win the War Within

In this last section we talked about the ways men handle challenges and battles—the good, the bad, and the ugly. We explored the secret of learning to master your mind—by capturing one thought at a time and giving it to God for alterations and repairs—as a way to win the war within, no matter what is happening around you.

• • •

Our prayer is that as you read, study, contemplate, and apply these seven vital lessons, you will discover the soul of a hero within your own mind and heart. May this book prepare you for the journey ahead, however long or short, however joyful or difficult, so that you may look back with deep satisfaction at a life well lived.

Not a perfect life.

Not a pain-free life.

The grace of God means something like: Here is your life.
You might never have been, but you are because the party
wouldn't have been complete without you. Here is the world.
Beautiful and terrible things will happen. Don't be afraid.
I am with you.

FREDERICK BUECHNER, *WISHFUL THINKING*

But a full life, rich with loving relationships, tears and laughter, courage in hard times, and a sense of wonder at all that is good. In a world that is surely not yet heaven, may you be a hero to those who have been privileged to know you. May you leave a trail of blessings and hope, a glimpse of God's great, wide, all-encompassing love, for others who will follow after you.

Now, go. Fly. Soar. Leap some tall buildings (or Lego towers) in a single bound.

God gave you life so you could fully live it. Yes, we know that your to-do lists are long and your calendar is full. But you're a hero in the making now, so try not to miss the stuff that matters most.

Thank you for reading *The Soul of a Hero*. Our hope is that God will use the biblical concepts in this book to provoke real change in the hearts of men. Our world is changing, and we can no longer go about our own masculine journey without some slight (or major) changes to how we view ourselves, the women in our lives, our friends, and (for those of us who have them) our sons.

It is for these last two—friends and sons—that we want to offer you a challenge.

If this content has proven helpful to you in your own journey, here are two ways to pass it along:

1. *One-on-one with a friend or your son.* Going through the stories and principles could make a real difference to someone who is still forming his views on manhood, still finding his purpose and his way, still learning how he should treat women in a way that honors God.
2. *With a small group of other men.* If you have a group of friends who will relate to this material— inside or outside the church—we firmly believe it will be a thought-provoking book to discuss.

I (Steve) was privileged to be one of the speakers at a recent Promise Keepers event, and I closed my talk with this challenge for men to take to heart.

God Does Not Want Us to Walk in Shame
Repeat this, if you believe it:
I am God's man
I have a calling on my life
I am called to a great purpose
I am called to be a hero in every man's battle
I am called to conquer every evil from without,
    and every excuse from within
I am called to make a difference
I am called to be God's man
I accept God's calling
I will live into it
I will live up to it
So help me, God

If you took this challenge, or if the book helped you along your path, we'd love to hear your thoughts. You can send an email to sarterburn@newlife.com.

In the battle together,
Steve and Dave

Notes

INTRODUCTION: HEROES AT HEART

1. See Isaiah 61:1 and Luke 4:18.
2. See Bruce K. Alexander, "The Myth of Drug-Induced Addiction," Senate of Canada, accessed October 1, 2020, https://sencanada.ca/content/sen /committee/371/ille/presentation/alexender-e.htm.
3. Howard Thurman, *The Living Wisdom of Howard Thurman: A Visionary for Our Time*, audio CD (Louisville, CO: Sounds True, 2010).
4. John 10:10
5. See Genesis 7:11.
6. See Genesis 6:22, 7:5.

1. COME EMPTY

1. To find out more about the "and more!" see Stephen and Misty Arterburn, *The Mediterranean Love Plan: Seven Secrets to Life-Long Passion in Marriage* (Grand Rapids, MI: Zondervan, 2017).
2. See Luke 5:1-9.
3. See Matthew 4:19; Mark 1:17; and Luke 5:10-11.
4. See Matthew 14:13-21; Mark 6:30-44; Luke 9:10-17; and John 6:1-15.
5. See John 2:1-11.
6. See 2 Corinthians 12:9.
7. Matthew 11:20
8. Matthew 11:25-26
9. Matthew 11:28
10. Matthew 19:14
11. C. S. Lewis, *The Lion, the Witch and the Wardrobe* (New York: HarperCollins, 1950), 139.

2. YOUR TRUE IDENTITY

1. See Genesis 3:1-24.
2. *Blue Bloods*, season 7, episode 22, "The Thin Blue Line," directed by David Barrett, written by Ian Biederman, aired May 5, 2017, https://www .amazon.com/gp/video/detail/B01KT9OFKM/ref=atv_dp_season_select _s7, 39:53–40:13.
3. 1 Peter 2:9, NIV
4. Judges 6:11
5. Judges 6:12
6. Judges 6:12
7. Judges 6:13
8. Judges 6:14, NIV
9. Judges 6:14, NIV
10. See 2 Peter 1:3.
11. See Judges 7:16-22 and 8:10.
12. Nouwen wrote a book on the same topic, which we highly recommend: *The Return of the Prodigal Son: A Story of Homecoming* (New York: Image Books, 1994).
13. See Matthew 4:1-11; Mark 1:11-13; and Luke 4:1-14.
14. See Ephesians 1:3-23.
15. Colossians 3:3, NIV
16. Matthew 3:17, NIV
17. 2 Corinthians 4:9
18. Henri J. M. Nouwen, *Life of the Beloved: Spiritual Living in a Secular World* (London: Hodder & Stoughton, 1993), 28, 30, 49.
19. Brennan Manning with John Blase, *All Is Grace: A Ragamuffin Memoir* (Colorado Springs: David C Cook, 2011), 192.
20. John 15:4, ESV
21. Job 1:21, paraphrased from the King James Version
22. Romans 8:38
23. See Matthew 16:13-20.
24. See Luke 22:54-57; Mark 14:69-70; Matthew 26:73-75; Luke 22:59-62; and John 18:13-27.
25. See John 21:15-17.
26. The phrase "strong at the broken places" comes from Ernest Hemingway, *A Farewell to Arms* (New York: Scribner, 2014), 216.

3. THE DAD FACTOR

1. Tim Madigan is not the journalist featured in the 2019 movie *A Beautiful Day in the Neighborhood*. That was Tom Junod of *Esquire* magazine.

2. Tim Madigan, *I'm Proud of You: My Friendship with Fred Rogers* (Los Angeles: Ubuntu, 2012), 50.

3. Madigan, *I'm Proud of You*, 41.

4. Madigan, *I'm Proud of You*, 4.

5. Fred Rogers, *The World according to Mister Rogers: Important Things to Remember* (New York: Hyperion, 2003), 88. Italics in the original.

6. Jim Daly with Bob DeMoss, *Finding Home: An Imperfect Path to Faith and Family* (Colorado Springs: David C Cook, 2007), 210. Italics in the original.

7. Italics added.

4. SIDEKICKS FOR THE SOUL JOURNEY

1. Don Malarkey with Bob Welch, *Easy Company Soldier* (New York: St. Martin's Press, 2008), 184.

2. Malarkey, *Easy Company Soldier*, 184.

3. Malarkey, *Easy Company Soldier*, 184.

4. Geoffrey L. Greif, *Buddy System: Understanding Male Friendships* (New York: Oxford University Press, 2009), 6.

5. Jeffrey Zaslow, "Friendship for Guys (No Tears!)," *Wall Street Journal*, April 7, 2010, https://www.wsj.com/articles/SB10001424052702304620304575166090090482912.

6. Jim Rohn, "A Good Life Contains These 6 Essentials," Jim Rohn International, January 31, 2019, https://www.jimrohn.com/good-life-essentials/.

7. For example, see "Can Relationships Boost Longevity and Well-Being?" *Harvard Health Letter*, June 2016, https://www.health.harvard.edu/mental-health/can-relationships-boost-longevity-and-well-being.

8. Ron Hall and Denver Moore with Lynn Vincent, *Same Kind of Different as Me* (Nashville: W Publishing, 2016), 107.

9. Donald Miller, *Scary Close: Dropping the Act and Finding True Intimacy* (Nashville: Nelson Books, 2014), 45.

10. Heather Kopp, *Sober Mercies: How Love Caught Up with a Christian Drunk* (New York: Jericho Books, 2013), 81.

11. Heather Kopp, "When Shared Brokenness Trumps Shared Beliefs," *HuffPost*, updated December 6, 2017, https://www.huffpost.com/entry/bonding-over-brokenness-v_b_5247781.

12. Ken Blanchard, *Catch People Doing Something Right* (n.p.: Executive Excellence, 1999).

13. Acts 4:36

14. 1 Thessalonians 5:11

15. David Gleeson, Stephen Beresford, *Tolkien*, directed by Dome Karukoski (2019; Los Angeles, CA: Searchlight Pictures). See also https://www.movie quotesandmore.com/tolkien-best-movie-quotes/.

16. C. S. Lewis, *The Four Loves* (San Diego: Harcourt Brace Jovanovich, 1960), 116.

17. According to the popular website 14ers.com, "To be ranked, a peak must rise at least 300 feet above the saddle that connects it to the nearest 14er peak (if another exists nearby). This guideline has been in use in Colorado for some time. [Five] peaks are not ranked because they do not fit this criteria, but they are . . . named and recognized on USGS maps."

18. Edwin Markham, "Outwitted," in *The Shoes of Happiness and Other Poems* (Garden City, NY: Doubleday, Page & Co., 1915), 1.

19. ESV

5. YOUR MISSION, SHOULD YOU CHOOSE TO ACCEPT IT

1. Luke 2:52

2. Rick Warren, *The Purpose Driven Life* (Grand Rapids, MI: Zondervan, 2002), 30.

3. Lachlan Forrow, in foreword to Albert Schweitzer, *Out of My Life and Thought: An Autobiography*, 60th anniversary edition (Baltimore: Johns Hopkins University Press, 2009), viii.

4. Schweitzer, *Out of My Life and Thought*, viii.

5. "Athletic Award Is Presented to Ed Champion," *Carrol Daily Times Herald*, May 25, 1954, 7, column 1. See https://quoteinvestigator. com/2017/12/20/talent/#return-note-17584-1.

6. Frederick Buechner, *Wishful Thinking: A Theological ABC* (New York: Harper & Row, 1973), 95.

7. Colossians 3:23-24, ESV

8. NIV

9. Brother Lawrence, *The Practice of the Presence of God* (London: H. R. Allenson, 1906), 22.

10. See Luke 21:1-4.

6. BEING A REAL MAN IN #METOO TIMES

1. For the full story, see the book of Esther.

2. The five female prophets identified in the Old Testament are Miriam (Exodus 15:20), Deborah (Judges 4:4), Huldah (2 Kings 22:14 and 2 Chronicles 34:22), Noadiah (Nehemiah 6:14), and Isaiah's wife, "the prophetess" (Isaiah 8:3).

3. For the story of Deborah, Barak, Sisera, and Jael, see Judges 4–5.

4. See Tony Dungy, *Quiet Strength: The Principles, Practices, and Priorities of a Winning Life* (Carol Stream, IL: Tyndale House, 2007).

5. Abigail Adams, "Letter from Abigail Adams to John Adams, 31 March 31–5 April 1776," Massachusetts Historical Society, accessed October 15, 2020, https://www.masshist.org/digitaladams/archive/doc?id=L17760331aa.

6. John Adams, "Letter from John Adams to Abigail Adams, 14 April 1776," Massachusetts Historical Society, accessed October 15, 2020, https://www.masshist.org/digitaladams/archive/doc?id=L17760414ja.

7. Abigail Adams, "Letter from Abigail Adams to John Adams, 23 December 1782," Massachusetts Historical Society, accessed October 15, 2020, https://www.masshist.org/digitaladams/archive/doc?id=L17821223aa&bc=%2Fdigitaladams%2Farchive%2Fbrowse%2Fletters_1779_1789.php.

8. Kyle Benson, "Emotionally Intelligent Husbands Are Key to a Lasting Marriage," The Gottman Institute, October 7, 2016, https://www.gottman.com/blog/emotionally-intelligent-husbands-key-lasting-marriage/#:~:text=Developing%20emotional%20intelligence%20is%20the,dynamic%20will%20result%20in%20gridlock.

9. Benson, "Emotionally Intelligent Husbands."

10. Nicole Fisher, "Strong Father-Daughter Relationships Lead to Healthier, Happier Women," *Forbes*, June 21, 2020, https://www.forbes.com/sites/nicolefisher/2020/06/21/strong-father-daughter-relationships-lead-to-healthier-happier-women/#18d657672b63. See also Linda Nielsen, *Improving Father-Daughter Relationships: A Guide for Women and Their Dads* (New York: Routledge, 2020).

11. Linda Nielsen, "How Dads Affect Their Daughters into Adulthood," Institute for Family Studies blog, June 3, 2014, https://ifstudies.org/blog/how-dads-affect-their-daughters-into-adulthood.

12. Fisher, "Strong Father-Daughter Relationships."

13. Nielsen, "How Dads Affect Their Daughters."

14. Nielsen, "How Dads Affect Their Daughters."

15. Nielsen, "How Dads Affect Their Daughters."

16. Peggy Noonan, "John Paul II's Prescient 1995 Letter to Women," *Wall Street Journal*, November 30, 2017, Opinion, https://www.wsj.com/articles/john-paul-iis-prescient-1995-letter-to-women-1512086999.

17. Abigail Sanchez, "Beth Moore, Rick Warren & Kay Warren Discuss the Cost and Healing of Sexual Abuse," HelloChristian.com, January 30, 2018, https://hellochristian.com/11190-beth-moore-rick-warren-kay-warren-discuss-the-cost-and-healing-of-sexual-abuse.

18. Beth Moore, speaking at Reflections: A GC2 Summit on Responding to Sexual Harassment, Abuse, and Violence, Wheaton, Illinois, December 13, 2018. Quoted in Morgan Lee, "Max Lucado Reveals Past Sexual Abuse at Evangelical #MeToo Summit," *Christianity Today*, December 13, 2018, https://www.christianitytoday.com/news/2018/december/metoo -evangelicals-abuse-beth-moore-caine-lucado-gc2-summit.html.

19. Max Lucado, speaking at Reflections: A GC2 Summit on Responding to Sexual Harassment, Abuse, and Violence, Wheaton, Illinois, December 13, 2018. Quoted in Morgan Lee, "Max Lucado Reveals Past Sexual Abuse at Evangelical #MeToo Summit," *Christianity Today*, December 13, 2018, https://www.christianitytoday.com/news/2018/december/metoo -evangelicals-abuse-beth-moore-caine-lucado-gc2-summit.html.

20. See, for example, Ann Buchanan, *Cycles of Child Maltreatment: Facts, Fallacies and Interventions* (Wiley, 1996).

21. See John 8:1-11.

22. Matthew 26:10, NIV

23. See Matthew 26:13.

24. See John 4:4-26; Luke 10:38-42; John 11:1-44; Mark 15:40-41; John 19:25-27; Matthew 26:12; Mark 16:1; Matthew 28:1-10.

25. This quote is often attributed to Gloria Steinem, but in 2000 Steinem herself attributed it to writer Irina Dunn in a letter to the editors of *Time* magazine. See "Happy 80th Birthday Gloria Steinem: 8 of Her Funniest Quips," *Time*, March 25, 2014, https://time.com/36046 /gloria-steinem-8-funny-quotes-80-birthday/.

26. See John M. Gottman and Nan Silver, *The Seven Principles for Making Marriage Work: A Practical Guide from the Country's Foremost Relationship Expert* (New York: Three Rivers Press, 1999), 189–190; and Jon Beaty, "2 Biases That May Be Hurting Your Relationship," The Gottman Institute, July 7, 2017, https://www.gottman.com/blog/2-biases-may -hurting-relationship/.

27. Proverbs 31:10-11, 28, 31, NIV

7. MASTERING YOUR MIND

1. M. Scott Peck, *The Road Less Traveled*, 25th Anniversary Edition (New York: Touchstone, 2003), 15.

2. George Dawson and Richard Glaubman, *Life Is So Good: One Man's Extraordinary Journey through the Twentieth Century and How He Learned to Read at Age 98* (New York: Penguin Books, 201), 246, 259.

3. Hebrews 12:2, ESV

4. Johnny Dodd, "John McCain Tells PEOPLE How He Survived His 5 Years as a POW: 'Faith in God, My Fellow Prisoners, and My Country'" *People*, July 29, 2017, https://people.com/politics/john-mccain-pow -vietnam-story/.
5. 2 Corinthians 4:17, NIV
6. J. R. R. Tolkien, *The Return of the King* (New York: Ballantine, 2012), 211.
7. Luke 5:16, NASB
8. See Philippians 4:13.
9. Michael J. Fox, interview with Scott Raab, *Esquire*, January 1, 2008, https:// classic.esquire.com/article/2008/1/1/what-ive-learned-michael-j-fox.
10. 2 Corinthians 4:16, ESV
11. Romans 12:2, NIV; 2 Corinthians 10:5, NKJV
12. NIV
13. John 8:32, NIV
14. See John 14:6.
15. John 8:36, NIV
16. Julian of Norwich, *Revelation of Love*, trans. and ed. John Skinner (New York: Image Books, 1997), 55.

8. GET READY TO SOAR

1. Christopher Reeve, *Still Me* (New York: Ballantine Books, 1999), 267.
2. Tom Hanks, as Jimmy Dugan in *A League of Their Own*, Columbia Pictures, 1992; "A League of Their Own—The Hard Is What Makes It Great.m4v," jonelski, YouTube video, 1:37–1:45, https://www.youtube .com/watch?v=ndL7y0MIRE4.

About the Authors

Stephen Arterburn is the founder and chairman of New Life Ministries—the nation's largest faith-based broadcast, counseling, and treatment ministry—and host of the *New Life Live!* broadcast. Steve is the author and coauthor of more than one hundred books, with twelve million in print, including *Every Man's Battle* and the *The Life Recovery Bible*, which he edited with David Stoop. Steve also founded the Women of Faith conferences, attended by more than five million women. Steve and his family live in Carmel, Indiana, where he serves as the teaching pastor of one of the largest churches in America, Northview Church.

David Stoop, PhD, is a licensed clinical psychologist in California. He received a master's in theology from Fuller Theological Seminary and a doctorate from the University of Southern California. He is frequently heard as a cohost on the nationally syndicated *New Life Live!* radio and TV program. David is the founder and director of the Center for Family

Therapy in Newport Beach, California. He is also an adjunct professor at Fuller Seminary and serves on the executive board of the American Association of Christian Counselors. David is a Gold Medallion–winning author and has written more than thirty books, including *Forgiving the Unforgivable* and *Rethink How You Think*. He and his wife, Jan, live in Newport Beach, California, and have three sons and six grandchildren.

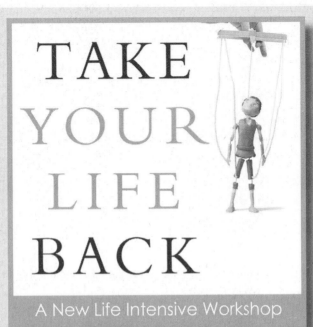

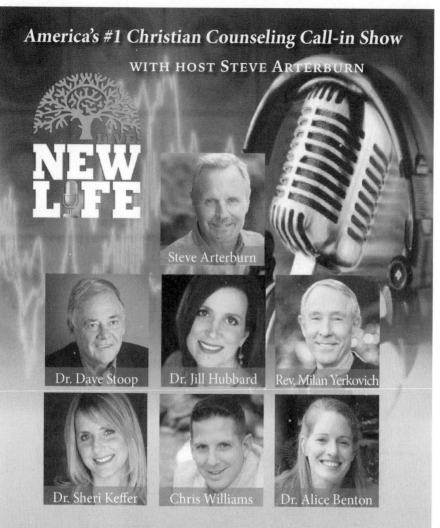

A Bible for Every Battle
Every Man Faces

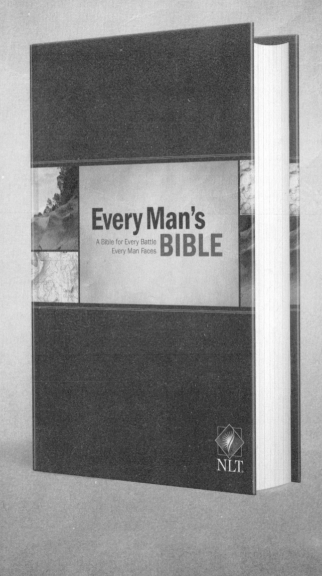